Mount Batten

The Flying Boats of Plymouth

Mount Batten

The Flying Boats of Plymouth

GERALD WASLEY

First published in Great Britain in 2006

For Maria Jane

British Library Cataloguing-in-Publication Data.
A CIP record for this title is available from the British Library.

ISBN 1 84114 495 9
ISBN 978 1 84114 495 5

HALSGROVE

Halsgrove House
Lower Moor Way
Tiverton, Devon EX16 6SS
Tel: 01884 243242
Fax: 01884 243325
Email: sales@halsgrove.com
Website: www.halsgrove.com

Title page photograph: *A picture taken from the Citadel of seven Sunderland flying boats anchored in the Cattewater. It is believed the photograph was taken in the immediate postwar period.*

Printed and bound in Great Britain by CPI Bath.

*Whilst every care has been taken to ensure the accuracy of the information
contained in this book, the publisher disclaims responsibility for any mistakes which
may have been inadvertently included.*

Acknowledgements

Writing a book is always an undertaking that requires the help and goodwill of many people when researching and preparing the text and images. The process involved in creating *Mount Batten – The Flying Boats of Plymouth* is no exception. Listing names on a page to acknowledge help received does not quantify the assistance I was given. I thank all the individuals and organisations listed below and are very grateful for their contribution. One of the bonuses in writing a book is the number of kind people one comes into contact with.

Norman Ash; Australian War Memorial Archives; British Library; British Newspaper Library in London; British Overseas Aircraft Corporation; Bryan Benge; John Buckingham; Bill Cole; Exeter Police Museum; Fleet Air Arm Museum at Yelverton; the late P. Ghillyer; Mrs D. Harris; Yvonne Hibbert; Mrs T. Hugo; Central Library at Hull; David Hunt; Imperial War Museum in London; Darrell Jago; Barbara Lang; Stuart Leslie; Peter London; Wing Commander Mahon; Moseley Library; National Archives at Kew; the late David Murch; Local History Studies Library in Plymouth; Plymouth City Museum & Art Gallery; RAF Museum at Hendon; Barbara Mickley; Oxford University Committee for Archaeology; *Plymouth Evening Herald*; Radford and Hooe Lake Preservation Society; Revd Ian Provost; the *Western Morning News*; Mary Outhwaite; D. Pascho; Mrs Ridgeway; Mrs M. Rowe; Paul Skentelbery; Mary Skilton; St John's Church, Hooe; Staddon Heights Golf Club; Surcouf internet group; Mrs Dennis Teague; University of Texas, Austin; West Country Views; Patsy Wilkens; George Williams; Mrs Sheila White; June Whyte; Helen Yate.

Preface

This book is a history of Mount Batten, which is part of the city of Plymouth and the parish of Plymstock. The core of the text is about the marine aviation presence that covered a period of 75 years. The first chapter, however, refers to the ancient history of the peninsular, a subject that has been written about before, but to exclude it I feel would make the text incomplete. Using contemporary images, I have in Chapter 2, given the reader an insight into how the flying boat station that was built altered the appearance of Mount Batten forevermore. This chapter also describes the station's activities during the First World War and gives fascinating glimpses of the designs of the seaplanes associated with the base. From Mount Batten the gallant airmen flew their seaplanes, engaged in a relentless war against the German U-boats that were causing havoc to Allied shipping. The book reveals that immediately after the war the Air Ministry had plans for Mount Batten to become a permanent flying boat base.

Chapter 3 describes how Mount Batten, although not operational, contributed to aviation history with the many pioneering flights that started from the Cattewater. It is interesting to study the pictures of the aircraft to see how the design and performance of aircraft changed over the years. A chapter has been included on the presence of the legendary aircraftman, T.E. Shaw (Lawrence of Arabia) who was stationed at Mount Batten in the early 1930s. In spite of the considerable material that has been written about Lawrence, very little has ever been published before about his life at Mount Batten.

Mount Batten in the Second World War focuses on the airmen of the Royal Australian Air Force who flew the magnificent Short Sunderland flying boats on patrols deep into the Western Approaches and the Bay of Biscay. Many of these men lost their lives. Their names are remembered in the St John's Church at Hooe. When the airmen warriors had returned to Australia, Mount Batten became a base for Marine craft. Chapter 6 describes the postwar years, including the official closure of the RAF base.

Mount Batten can be thought of as being reborn when through the Plymouth Development Corporation it became a public domain. Whatever the benefits to the local economy the commercialisation of parts of Mount Batten has achieved and the public facilities that are enjoyed, perhaps the most interesting part of the recent history of the area is the establishment of a small community on this ancient land. The last chapter, therefore, includes aspects of the history of the Cattewater villages as these communities are linked irrevocably with Mount Batten. Although I felt it was necessary to write about these villages there is no attempt on my part to present it as a definitive history.

What is remarkable is that the 75 years of aviation history at Mount Batten has never been part of Plymouth's heritage. I hope in some small way I have redressed this balance.

G.D. Wasley, 2006

Contents

The Spanish Armada in crescent formation prior to passing Plymouth. What is interesting in this famous Robert Adams chart is the line of English warships sailing out from the Cattewater to confront the enemy.

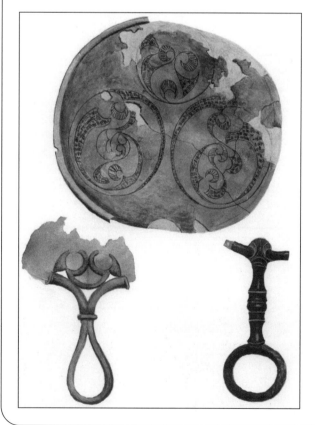

Illustrations of a late-Iron-Age decorated bronze mirror back and mirror handles discovered in the Stamford Hill cemetery. These were some of the finds revealed when Stamford Fort was near completion. Unfortunately the mirror was destroyed during the Plymouth Blitz of the 1940s.

Chapter 1

Mount Batten Peninsula

Early History and Archaeology

Mount Batten, situated at the mouth of the River Plym (Cattewater) in the parish of Plymstock, is part of the city of Plymouth. The popular image of Mount Batten is of an ancient round tower that stands on a large rock, but it is more than this; Mount Batten is a peninsula. Once a picturesque promontory depicted by many artists including Turner, its headland was ravished in the nineteenth century by quarrying. Whatever appealing features remained were then marred by the military buildings that stood there for over 70 years. Yet because of its unique location and history it is a fascinating place to visit. T.E. Lawrence, writing to one of his friends, describes Mount Batten 'like a fossil lizard stretched out into the Sound with its head towards Plymouth and its root in golf-links' (no longer at Batten) which are a cascade of green lawns. There is, however, considerable natural beauty close by with the rolling hills that border the South Hams. In addition there are the cliff tops at Staddon Heights above Mount Batten, which offer a glorious panorama that embraces the waters of Plymouth Sound and the landscapes of east Cornwall and Plymouth Hoe.

When people stand on the ancient ground of Mount Batten and look across the Cattewater, they are at the scene of some highly important historic events associated with the history of English-speaking people. Here in the waters of Clovelly Bay, the anchored warships of the English Fleet waited for the order to sail out from Plymouth Sound into the English Channel to confront the mighty Spanish Armada that had arrived to threaten the very existence of England. If on 6 September 1620 anyone was on Mount Batten they would have seen the Pilgrim Fathers on the *Mayflower* set out from Sutton Harbour on their adventure across the Atlantic Ocean. As time went by, it was from this same harbour that other ships departed as they transported more emigrants to colonise the countries of the British Empire.

Man's systematic industrialisation of Plymouth and its surrounding area revealed Mount Batten as a site of international archaeological importance. The quarrying and the construction of the military buildings at Mount Batten, while destroying the natural contours of the headland exposed a wide range of late prehistoric and Roman material covering a period from the ninth century BC to the fourth century AD. During the quarrying at Mount Batten in 1830 two hoards of Celtic coins were discovered, which indicated that there had been an Iron Age settlement in the area. Some 30 years later, during the construction of Fort Stamford, an Iron Age cemetery was discovered. Among many of the interesting items found in these graves was part of a beautiful bronze engraved mirror. Sadly the mirror, along with other archaeological finds discovered on the peninsula, were destroyed in the Plymouth Blitz during the Second World War. Other items that were found are deposited at Plymouth's City Museum and at Oxford. In the late-nineteenth century the 'Batten Skull' was found at Kelly's shipbuilding yard. This item was the subject of much interest at a meeting in 1891 of the Plymouth Institution. The body of the person, believed to have been a middle-aged woman, was buried in an upright crouching position. It is thought the remains date from Neolithic times, approximately 2000BC, and resemble the Welsh Neolithic cave folk. Various finds indicate prehistoric people settled at Mount Batten peninsula and sometime later the area was a Roman trading post. On Staddon Heights, which overlook Mount Batten, the recent discovery of the foundations of a Bronze Age round house is further evidence of ancient inhabitation.

During the construction of the flying boat station during the First World War, Roman coins, a Roman dagger, an axe and pottery fragments were found, along with other Roman remains including some small bronze heads that probably decorated a lady's casket. Other historic items were recovered from the beach, having been discarded by workmen, although some of the men were known to keep their findings and sell them to interested parties.

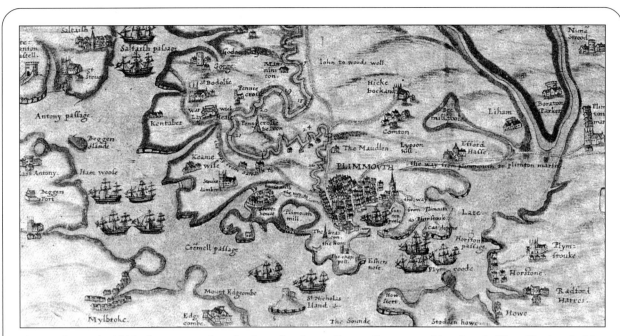

A map drawn in 1591, three years after the Armada, shows the small communities close to How Stert and ships anchored in the Cattewater.

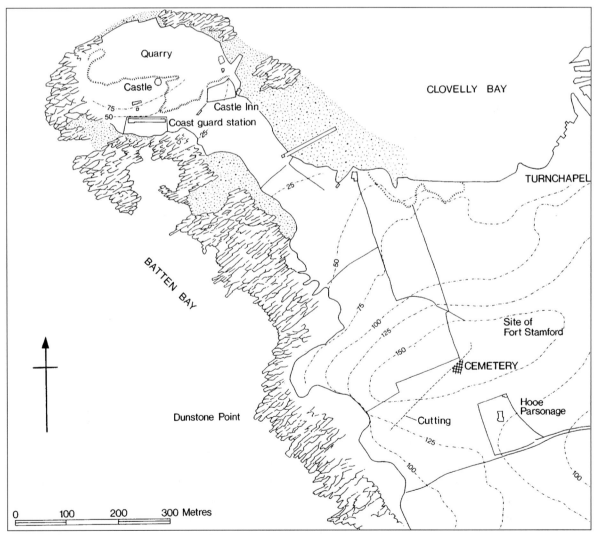

A diagram of Mount Batten peninsula showing the site of the late-Iron-Age or Roman-period cemetery discovered in 1863 on Stamford Hill during the construction of the artillery fort.

After the Second World War the general consensus was that there was no further historical information to be obtained from excavation. The ancient history of Mount Batten, however, interested Terry Hugo, a civilian employee in charge of catering at RAF Mount Batten. He began reading books and papers on the subject, which led him to probe into the nature of the ground disturbances to discover if there was still any surviving midden material. Finds that he made were taken to Plymouth's City Museum for identification. This attracted the interest of Plymouth archaeologists and resulted in the Institute of Archaeology at the University of Oxford becoming involved. Permission to excavate was given by the Commanding Officer of RAF Mount Batten. Through Terry Hugo's interest and initiative, the archaeology of Mount Batten was transformed.

A trial excavation began in 1983. A trench was made close to one of the aircraft hangars. The next season a team of archaeologists from Oxford began excavation. The finds included numerous fragments of bronze objects including a phalera (a bright metal disc worn on the chest as an ornament by men), a bracelet and a brooch.

Lack of evidence concerning Mount Batten from the post-Roman period up to medieval times means there is something of a void in the area's history. It is thought that Mount Batten was left to the natural elements for around 1,000 years, only occupied by whatever living creatures had made their way to the area. The only known documentary history we have from this period reveals a manor of Hooe was extant in the twelfth and thirteenth centuries but to what extent Mount Batten was part of this manor is not known.

During the summer of 1580, the year Francis Drake returned to Plymouth from circumnavigating the world, the seaport was in the grips of the plague. The epidemic was so severe that the choosing of the Mayor of Plymouth was held outside the town at Cattedown. The visitation of the Black Death resulted in many of the townspeople dying; one record quotes a figure of 2,000 people. The total population of Plymouth at the time could not have been much greater. The presence of the plague in Plymouth during 1580 caused a further exodus from the town, which left it defenceless.

The village of Plymstock just a few miles from Mount Batten suffered the plague in October 1591 when 46 people in the parish died within four months. The local Byrt family lost nine members.

It is conceivable that the plague was carried over from Plymouth by people who travelled on the Cattedown–Oreston ferry to Plymstock.

The history of Mount Batten takes a macabre turn during the time the plague raged in Plymouth. So-called 'pest houses' were erected at Mount Batten to isolate those people who were known to be infected with the disease. As there was no knowledge at the time of what caused the plague and certainly no remedy, it seems there was no alternative but to isolate the victims. These houses were not part of an established community, they simply provided rudimentary accommodation for the dying, rather than care and support. Plymouth sufferers of the plague were transported across the Cattewater to Batten and left to fend for themselves. Excavations at different times on Mount Batten peninsula have revealed the graves of some of these poor wretches.

The one time presence of plague victims and their buried corpses at Batten must have cast a fearful shadow over the area. One can imagine with superstition prevalent during this period that it was not a place to which people would want to venture.

It was not just Mount Batten that was affected in this way. In 1625 the Privy Council received notice of eight suspected plague deaths 'over at Osen', a seventeenth-century reference to Oreston.

Troubled Times

Mount Batten was associated with military matters from about the time of the Spanish Armada (1588). An invasion scare had caused Plymouth's defences to be strengthened and consideration was given to building a fort at Mount Batten. Two years after the defeat of the Armada there is a report of a 'barricade on Howstert'.

Between 1633 and 1634 the 'Batten Isthmus' was breached on both sides of the peninsula by the erosion of the sea and repairs were carried out to prevent further damage. However, the sea wall that was built to resolve the problem required further work on it two years later. Plymouth and Saltash were responsible for the management of the Cattewater. This included the annual removal of rubble and silt from the Cattewater, which was dumped on the narrow land on the south side of Mount Batten. It took almost another 250 years before the Mount Batten Breakwater was built to resolve this problem.

During the turbulent years of the Civil War (1642–46), Plymouth was under siege (1643–46) from

Royalist forces. Such a prolonged experience would have been the source of great strain for the villagers living in the Plymstock and Cattewater communities. The conflict was literally on their doorsteps. A Royalist force was stationed at Plymstock with troops at Hooe and Oreston.

The Parliamentarians built a fortification up on a hill near Mount Stamford. With all the military action going on in the area, both sides continually fought, ceded ground and then won it back. The local economy suffered as shipping was driven out of the Cattewater by a Royalist cannon mounted at Oreston. The importance of Mount Batten's link with the defence of Plymouth is reflected in the numerous maps that were drawn at this time showing Mount Batten peninsula. For example, there are maps that were prepared by the one-time enemies of the realm. These are of considerable interest to the local historian as they include place names and indicate the presence of small communities and military defences in the area. One seventeenth-century map names the Mount Batten headland 'Howe Stert', while other maps refer to it as 'Haw Stert' (meaning finger of land). This name has early origins – indeed it is recorded that Mount Batten was known as Hooe Stert in 1296.

In September 1644 the King Charles I's army launched an unsuccessful attack on Plymouth. Vice Admiral William Batten, who was for Plymouth, had already arrived and fortified Haw Stert. Subsequent fighting resulted in the Royalists abandoning the headland: it was after this action that the name Mount Batten was given to this area of land.

On 18 January 1646 the siege of Plymouth was finally raised by General Fairfax. The Civil War was over. Later King James II ordered the building of Plymouth's Royal Citadel. As there was now a fear of a Dutch invasion, a decision was made to build a round tower with embrasures for ten guns to protect Sutton Harbour. The stone to build the tower was most likely from Mount Batten. For many years the round tower was called Mount Batten Castle; its image became synonymous with the locality.

Before the Plymouth Breakwater was constructed, the ships that anchored in Plymouth Sound had no protection against the fierce gales that would sometimes force the vessels onto the rocks and drive them up the Cattewater – which could cause a loss of ships and life. Nicholas Pocock's dramatic 1811 painting (at the time of writing on display in a large exhibition of 'Maritime Paintings' in the Plymouth City Museum & Art Gallery) entitled *The East Indiaman 'Dutton' wrecked in Plymouth Sound* conveys the horror of the wreck which occurred on 26 January 1796. The *Dutton* hit the rocks near Mount Batten and lost her rudder. This meant she could not be steered, so she was forced onto the rocks under the Citadel. There were over 600 on board and miraculously most were saved due to the outstanding heroism and leadership of Captain Pellew, who by chance was travelling nearby in his carriage. He was later made Lord Exmouth. This event was considered rather newsworthy at the time and was the subject matter for a number of paintings, including work by Thomas Luny.

Starting in 1812, several hundred labourers took over 30 years to complete the breakwater, which was constructed from limestone, taken from the nearby Oreston quarries, and topped with granite.

Early in the nineteenth century, when England was at war with France, thousands of French prisoners were brought to Plymouth and placed in detention around Devon and Cornwall. Mount Batten, it is reported, became a prisoner-of-war camp where many Frenchman were buried.

Close to Mount Batten is Jennycliff, known at one time as Rum Bay, a place with an abundant source of fresh water that poured out of the cliff. At one time, water would be collected by mariners and taken back to the ships for drinking and mixed with tots of rum.

In an attempt to defeat the smuggling of goods ashore the Board of Customs established a coastguard service. From 1823 coastguard cottages were being built around Plymouth Sound. According to Gill, the Plymouth historian, coastguards were present at Mount Batten in 1850. A terrace of coastguard cottages facing out across Plymouth Sound was built at Mount Batten with each cottage having its own garden. The coastguards also had a hut between Batten and Jennycliff that they used when the weather was bad. Mount Batten's tower was also used as a coastguard watch-tower.

As the activities of the smugglers were slowly overcome, the role of the coastguards changed to watching for signs of vessels in distress at sea and launching rescue operations. Once a lifeboat station was established at Millbay Docks in the 1860s, the Mount Batten coastguards would, if a ship was sighted in distress, fire a rocket to signal that a lifeboat was needed. The rocket life-saving equipment was first kept at the rear of the coastguard cottages. As there were insufficient coastguards, a

To Robert Palmer Esq.

Whereas In Consequence of Copies of the Resolutions of the Mayor Capital Burgesses Common Council Men Merchants and Inhabitants of the Borough of Plymouth held at the Guildhall at Plymouth on Thursday the Thirteenth day of February instant (Transmitted to the Portreeve of Tavistock) for taking into consideration a Petition of Stephen Drew and William Dunsterville Esquires. then and now before a Committee of the House of Commons. for Cleansing and Preserving the Harbour of Catwater and granting to them an Impost of Tonnage. Who Resolved

That the Plan proposed by the Petitioners was highly injurious to the Public and particularly to the Inhabitants of that Borough having a direct Tendency to lessen the Trade of that Port.

That the Opinion of that Meeting was that if the said Plan should take effect it would tend only to the private Emolument of Individuals. by vesting in them a perpetual Right of Ballasting the Royal Navy and the Trading Vessells frequenting the Port to the prejudice of the Public.

That should it be necessary to build a Fence at Mount Batton and remove the Middle Bank in Catwater in Order to render the Harbour more commodious

your utmost Endeavours to prevent the Bill being carried into a Law.

Signed by 310 Persons.

In 1783 a scheme was proposed for the dredging and improving of the Cattewater, that part of the River Plym adjacent to Lord Morley's land. The inhabitants of Plymouth strongly objected as income from trade would accrue to the landowners.

A late-nineteenth-century map.

Mount Batten beach and the Cattewater during the late-nineteenth century. In the foreground is the slipway of Kelly's shipyard with Plymouth in the background. A white-walled building with a central chimney-stack, behind the masts of the beached vessel, stands close to the waterfront facing a small harbour.

coastguard auxiliary was formed with a purpose-built rocket house (which is still there) above Turnchapel. Once the coastguard cottages became defunct, they were sold. June Whyte, a local historian from Hooe, recalls her great-grandparents rented one of the cottages and used it as a place to relax. They would travel down to Mount Batten from Oreston by pony and trap. A relation of Isaac Foot, a Liberal Plymouth politician, also used one of the cottages as a summer residence.

Development of the Area

Significant changes occurred with quarrying at Mount Batten (and the other Cattewater villages) starting in the early part of the nineteenth century. As new quarry areas were exploited so parts of the foreshore had quays and slipways constructed to transport the stone. In 1839 Lord Morley issued a license to search for iron ore around Mount Batten. Iron was found and shipments began to a smelting house at Neath in South Wales. However, the material was of poor quality and after three years the mine was abandoned. Some years later, when the lease was being sold, an advertisement in the *Mining Journal* described the ore of yielding 57 per cent metallic iron.

A Peter Simmons had control of the quarry by 1841 and supplied large quantities of stone to the Admiralty for the building of the Keyham steam yards at Devonport Dockyard. A petition was submitted to the Admiralty by 53 leading citizens that resulted in an agreement between the Admiralty

and Lord Morley, the landowner, that imposed restrictions on quarrying. A consequence of this was that the ancient round tower was saved from possible destruction, as the removal of stone in this the sector where the tower stood would have undermined the foundations of the structure. However, the exploitation of stone at Mount Batten continued until the mid-1860s, when quarrying in the area was starting to tail off.

Quarrying was not the only commercial activity that had been carried on at Mount Batten. There are records of boat building at Batten during the middle of the nineteenth century. William Routleff had a shipyard at Mount Batten in the 1850s. Here the 200 tons *Countess of Morley* was launched. The second Saltash chain ferry was built there in 1851 and the rigged sloop *Batten Castle* was also constructed there. Routleff's shipyard was taken over by W.S. Kelly who had moved from Dartmouth, and continued to build various types of boats until the beginning of the twentieth century. *Alfred Rooker* was the last ship built by Kelly in 1878. Later she was converted at Oreston for Arctic work.

Kelly's shipyard was not the only one at Mount Batten. John and Isaac Darton built ships next to Kelly's yard, among them was at least one of the ships of the Oreston and Steamship Company. John Pope, who owned a Turnchapel boatyard, is recorded in a 1856 Cattewater chart to have a dock at Mount Batten referred to as 'Popes Old Dock'. The Oreston and Turnchapel Steamboat Company's founder, Henry Elford, had a boat in his ferry fleet, the *Rapid*, that served the Cattewater villagers for a number of years. This vessel was built at Mount Batten.

Visitors Come to Mount Batten

Although Mount Batten is close to Plymouth, separated by a channel of water, the high-density housing and other buildings of the town contrasted sharply with the green expanse of Mount Batten. No wonder that it was popular with Plymouthians who could come to Mount Batten and escape for a while from their drab surroundings and enjoy some simple relaxation. Prior to the introduction of Henry Elford's ferry service in the form of the Oreston and Turnchapel Steamboat Company (founded 1871), that linked Plymouth Barbican with Turnchapel, Oreston and Mount Batten there had been a number of small ferry boats that carried passengers from the Cattewater villages to various places around

Above: *The second Castle Inn (pictured) stood just left of where the entrance to the Mount Batten Centre is located. Note the washing jugs in each of the three open bedroom windows. The inn was a place not only for drinking beer, people also came for other refreshments. It was demolished in 1962.*

Left: *George Hine (centre) was once landlord of the Castle Inn, Mount Batten. One of his descendants supplied the author with pictures to use in this book. The man on the right of the picture is Robert Barlace, a Turnchapel shipbuilder. The other man is Samuel Rowe, School Attendance Officer. Other Castle Inn landlords included J.H. Watts and F.T. Webb.*

A late-nineteenth-century picture of Mount Batten and the Cattewater where Lord Boringdon of Saltram had laid mooring chains. In 1880 the Cattewater was handling a huge amount of trade from all over the world.

Although strewn with rocks and pebbles, the small sandy beach at Mount Batten facing out towards Plymouth Sound was a popular venue for the local Victorians and Edwardians.

This postcard of Mount Batten was sent by Sergeant William Perry to his sister and future brother-in-law who owned Fanshaw Farm and Tea Gardens at Hooe. Sergeant Perry was at the time stationed with the Royal Medical Corps at Stamford Fort. William Perry's son-in-law was Revd George Ridgway, the Padre at RAF Mount Batten during the Second World War.

This solid limestone building with brick quoins was built in 1834. Plymouth Fish Guano and Oil Company and then Climo Works used the building to make fish fertiliser from the dogfish waste of Plymouth's fish market.

Instead of being demolished by Plymouth Development Corporation the fish fertiliser factory was refurbished and is now a hotel and public house. It stands almost opposite the Mount Batten ferry pier.

Plymouth. Among them were *The Little Pet* used by the Oreston Steamboat Company and *The Favourite* that was built by Alfred Barlace, shipbuilder of Turnchapel. Both vessels were built in 1869.

A landing-stage at Mount Batten was used for the ferry passengers. In 1908 a pontoon and bridge were constructed at Batten to connect with the landing-stage. These structures enabled the steam ferries to disembark passengers at low tide.

The original Castle Inn at Mount Batten was built, it is recorded, to provide accommodation for men engaged in quarrying. This building was replaced by the second Castle Inn, that was sited nearer the shore. This was also frequented by the local quarry-men and then became popular with visitors to the area, as teas were served outside the premises with swings provided for the children. George Hine was, during Queen Victoria's reign one of the publicans of the Castle Inn. He is buried in St John's churchyard and some of his descendants still live in the area.

Although the Cattewater villages had their own public houses, villagers would make their way over to Mount Batten where there were two public houses – the Castle Inn and the Breakwater Inn. An early-twentieth-century journalist at the *Western Morning News*, R.V. Walling, described Mount Batten and its beach as attracting people to come over on the ferry boats from Phoenix Wharf to Turnchapel, or be rowed over by watermen, from where they would walk up the hill and down to the headland.

In April 1878 work started on constructing the Mount Batten Breakwater, which was completed three years later. The expenses needed to maintain the breakwater were met by a levy imposed by the Cattewater Commissioners, who were responsible for managing the shipping in the Cattewater.

At the end of the nineteenth century when the railway branch line from Plymouth to Turnchapel was opened. more people were encouraged to to visit the Mount Batten area. At Jennycliff a large bell tent was erected at weekends, from where refreshments were sold to the public. As Mount Batten became ever more popular, traders set up small stalls and there was even a Punch and Judy Show for the children who came to paddle in the water on the small sandy beach. Nearby the old coastguard cottages, there was also a large hut where a Mr and Mrs Andrews served teas. The hut could accommodate some 60 customers and would always appear to be full, with a queue waiting outside.

Whatever attractions enticed people to come to Mount Batten, a significant addition to the locality's outdoor life came about at the turn of the century. In 1903 (the year the Wright brothers made the first successful flight in an aeroplane) a nine-hole golf course was laid out on land between what is now St Luke's Hospice and the Jennycliff Café. The small clubhouse was situated at Mount Batten where 16 years later the flying boat station would be located. The golf club was later moved from Mount Batten to Staddon Heights. For many years the President of the United Services Golf Club was the Commander-in-Chief, Plymouth. At one time the golf club was financed by a compulsory levy upon all the officers' messes in the Plymouth area. The few non-commis-sioned servicemen who were permitted to play the course were not allowed to use the clubhouse and for a time there were no lady members. Any civilian member of the club was admitted by ballot by the officer members.

On Sunday 10 July 1904, thousands of people flocked to Plymouth Hoe to watch the arrival in Plymouth Sound of the huge German Imperial Fleet. People made their way to the cliffs at Staddon where they were able to get a good view of four of the German cruisers that had anchored in Jennycliff Bay. Two of these cruisers, the *Arcona* and the *Frauenlob*, would be sunk at the Battle of Jutland in 1916. People other than viewing the German warships would have seen HMS *Pique* moored in the bay. The *Pique* was a wood-built warship converted at Devonport Dockyard for use as a hospital ship. For years, if a ship entered Plymouth Sound with a crew member or a passenger suspected of having smallpox or any other infectious disease, he or she would be confined to the hospital ship. On 8 January 1908 a number of the crew of the SS *Dunbarmoor* that had arrived from Karachi were taken to the *Pique* suspected of suffer-ing from the plague. They were detained for three weeks until they were cleared of the disease. In 1910 the *Pique* was replaced by the *Flamingo*, a converted sloop, which remained moored in Jennycliff Bay until the 1930s. Thereafter anyone suspected of having an infectious disease was referred to the newly opened Lee Mill isolation hospital.

During one bank holiday in 1906, 10,000 people came by ferry to visit the Mount Batten area. Many of these local visitors would go further afield and make for Bovisand. People must have been deterred from visiting Mount Batten when a fish manure factory started up there in the years before the start of the First World War (pre-1914). Plymouth Fish

Mount Batten, c.1905, giving the impression of being a large field. The picture shows a number of people residing on the Cattewater side of Batten.

The Golf Clubhouse at Mount Batten close to the Cattewater. The road on the right of the picture led to the flying boat station, c.1924.

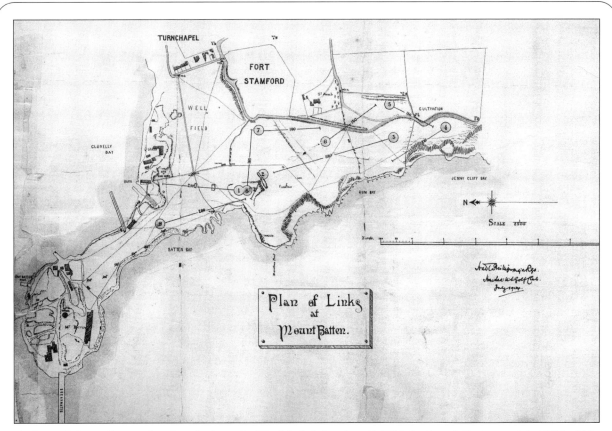

A plan of Mount Batten showing the layout of the United Services Golf Club when it first opened in 1904. Hole 9 can be seen well within the peninsula. The plan also indicates the extent of the Well Field that had five gates to gain entry.

A rare picture of golfers in the early 1920s. Each is wearing a tie, outside the clubhouse that was situated at Mount Batten.

Guano and Oil Company began making fertiliser at Mount Batten from the huge amount of dogfish waste that was being produced at the Barbican Fish Market. The stench was so bad that in 1912 an injunction was served to close down the factory. A by-law was passed forbidding the gutting of fish at the Barbican. This was not enforced, and consequently the Mount Batten factory revived its production and the dreadful smell that pervaded part of Plymouth continued until the Admiralty took over Mount Batten to establish the seaplane station.

Most of the fields of the hinterland close to Mount Batten were at one time part of Staddon Farm. On the Staddon slopes stood the old Hooe Rectory built above Staddon Fort. During the First World War the public were barred from the cliff tops, but with the coming of peace a wooden cabin on the beach down below was opened to serve teas. This service contin-

ued until 1989 when a storm washed the cabin away.

For many years Jennycliff was a popular place with people living in small caravans. Workers from the Devonport Dockyard arrived on the cliff tops of Jennycliff and began to build themselves wooden shacks, where they stayed at weekends and during the holidays. Eventually the local council issued an order for the shacks to be dismantled.

What happened at Mount Batten during the era of the flying boat is described in the following chapters. It seems that after the airmen had finally gone, history turned full circle – well almost – as Mount Batten appeared to be forsaken. One positive action that took place in this interim period was the building on high ground of St Luke's Hospice, which opened in 1982. Then through an injection of Government and EEC money, new plans were made and Mount Batten was born again.

Hooe Vicarage, c.1905, built just above the site of Stamford Fort. It was eventually taken over by the Ministry of Defence and used as officers' accommodation. A new vicarage was built in Turnchapel.

Chapter 2

The Royal Navy Air Station, Cattewater, 1917–18

The First World War radically changed the peaceful climate of Mount Batten, from a small headland of rock and grass with a few buildings and a slipway, to that of an important seaplane base that was needed as an additional force to protect allied convoys in the English Channel. It was instrumental in the detection and pursuit of U-boats that were causing havoc with allied shipping. Without our merchant ships the population of this country could have starved – and the Germans were aware of this. Ships were fairly regularly sunk off the southwest coast of England, although losses of shipping occurred in many other places around the UK.

Although it would not be until 1917 that Mount Batten officially opened as a seaplane station, there had been some aeronautical activity in the area prior to the war. A few months after the historic flight of the Wright brothers in 1903, the American Colonel S.F. Cody, had developed a man-carrying kite, that he claimed would be useful for military observation. Cody visited Plymouth to demonstrate to the Royal Navy how his kites could be used for anti-submarine duties. He was taken out in a warship to fly his kite in Plymouth Sound; contemporary photographs suggest he carried out his demonstration close to the Cattewater. The Royal Navy did not, however, put Cody's kite to any wartime use. Nevertheless, he remained in England, showing his kite and developing, with others, designs for such other aeronautical innovations as glider kites and planes with engines. He became one of the pioneers of British aviation.

Advances were being made in aircraft design and performance but the flying machines of the early-twentieth century were fragile and the performance

A Short Folder Admiralty 74-type biplane seaplane being hoisted aboard a Naval vessel. The aircraft was sent to Plymouth by rail in January 1914.

Above: *This historic picture shows the headland of Mount Batten before it was built on as a seaplane station. There being no roads or well-worn paths on the expanse of grass, it was a spacious environment that has been lost for ever. To the left are the old coastguard cottages with their white walled gardens.*

Left: *The pioneer aviator Colonel Cody wearing his 'Buffalo Bill Hat' demonstrating his man-lifting kite for the Royal Navy in Plymouth Sound in April 1904.*

This small fragile-looking seaplane is a Maurice-Farnam (No. 73) that arrived in Plymouth Sound in 1914 to assist in the location of the ill-fated submarine A7 that failed to surface while on trial from Devonport. This is possibly the earliest known seaplane associated with Plymouth. The picture was taken at Felixstowe.

of the engines were wanting; many of the pioneer pilots lost their lives due to the weak structure and unreliability of the machine they were flying. Aircraft accidents were common. There was, however, a developing interest in machine-powered flight. An English aviation pioneer, Claude Graham-White, suggested that aircraft would be useful as a weapon of war. He demonstrated how aircraft could be used in this way when he demonstrated attacking a warship when the British Fleet was reviewed by the King at Torquay during 1910. When a similar demonstration was given for the Army, British senior cavalry officers were not convinced of the role of the aeroplane as a military weapon and dismissed the idea claiming, 'the aircraft would frighten the horses'.

During this period, there were many private aviators flying their aircraft in the West Country. Aviation historian, the late Dennis Teague, records that a Mrs H. Hewlett flew a Maurice Farman biplane from Chelson Meadow, situated by the side of the River Plym, during August 1911. Designers had already started to be interested in aircraft that landed on the water, referred to as 'aquaplanes' and later known as seaplanes. Teague refers to seaplane trials being carried out in 1913 at a small site allocated near the fish guano fertiliser factory in Mount Batten. Whether this was associated with the Royal Flying Corps or Royal Navy has not been confirmed.

The earliest evidence of the presence of seaplanes at Plymouth is the arrival of a Maurice Farman seaplane (No. 73) in January 1914 that had flown from Grain, Kent, to assist in searching for the Devonport HM submarine A7 that, while on exercises, failed to surface off Rame Head, Cornwall. The presence of a Short Admiralty 74 Folder Tractor seaplane (with the propeller mounted at the front of the aircraft) that was sent by railway to Plymouth in January 1914 and remained there for three weeks, could also have been linked to the A7 disaster.

Over time, the British Government became aware of the potential use of aircraft as a weapon of war and recognised the need to form an Air Battalion (1911). A year later, in May 1912, the Royal Flying Corp (RFC) was formed. The newly established RFC had a military and naval wing under the control of the War Office and the Admiralty. The title of 'Naval Wing' was later dropped, and was replaced on 1 July 1914, just weeks before the outbreak of war, as a separate fighting force, the Royal Naval Air Service (RNAS). The role of the RNAS was to become extensive: other than carrying out coastal patrols and operations with the British Fleet in the forthcoming war, it would operate with the British Expeditionary Force on the continent and in other overseas theatres of war.

The capture of the Belgian Channel ports by the Germans in the early weeks of the First World War gave the enemy facilities in which to harbour their submarines. They were no longer compelled to return to their German bases. This meant there was an increasing threat to the UK's massive imports of material and food that were essential for the country to pursue the war and survive. That enemy submarines were now able to penetrate into the southwest of the English Channel was confirmed when, in the early hours of New Year's Day, 1915, the battleship HMS *Formidable* was torpedoed and sunk off Start Point. The warship went down with her captain and almost 600 officers and men. The German Admiralty, aware of the situation regarding the potential that existed in sinking allied shipping, issued a notice stating the waters in and out of the English Channel had been declared a war zone in which all allied shipping would be destroyed. Vessels from neutral countries would navigate these waters at their peril.

At the beginning of the German U-boat campaign the British Navy had few ideas of how to counter the submarine threat. For example, in the National Archives there is an official record of a naval officer's suggestion that when an enemy submarine's periscope was sighted, a boat should come alongside it, cover the periscope with a cloth, then shatter its glass with a hammer. An other idea was to train seagulls to sit on the periscope of a submarine.

As enemy incidents increased, a number of RNAS airship stations were established along the coastline of Britain. The British Admiralty introduced airship patrols using non-rigid airships for the purpose of spotting enemy submarines and floating mines, as well as performing escort duties in the shipping lanes. Airships were used in preference to aircraft at the time, as they were able to sustain flight for up to four hours and could, unlike aircraft, almost hover above a suspected target if the weather was favourable. Life for the airship crews was difficult and very uncomfortable as they were exposed to the elements in an open 'cockpit' for long periods of time. If there was any kind of accident or crew members were injured, the airship crews relied on good fortune to survive a forced landing.

In the summer of 1916, an airship station opened near Cury, close to the village of Mullion in Cornwall. This would become an important base for anti-

Laira substation (Chelson Meadow), c.1918. Behind the trees is Saltram House. Working with these airships was labour intensive as shown by the ground crew attempting to secure SSZ-42.

Airship SSE-2, built at Mullion and powered by twin Rolls-Royce engines, came down in the Cattewater while trying to land in a gale on Chelson Meadow, c.1918. The picture, taken from Mount Batten, shows the airship being retrieved.

submarine operations. The first airship patrol from RNAS Mullion was on 1 July. A week before, an airship making for Mullion crashed at Start Point killing three of its crew members. This date, 1 July 1916, was a significant day for another reason as it marked the start of the Battle of the Somme. These killing grounds resulted in tens of thousands of soldiers from both sides slaughtering each other. The *Western Express* reported that day 'very favourable war news continues to come'.

The Mullion airship patrols from Cornwall made their way along their designated routes, following a set pattern of flying up and down and across the Channel. To improve the patrol radius the Admiralty began to look for possible sites around the Plymouth area that would be suitable for the new type of smaller airship that had been introduced. A decision was taken that the most suitable site was at the racecourse at Chelson Meadow by the River Plym, close to the Cattewater. Here at this substation, RNAS Laira, the ground crew slept on the benches in the racecourse stand. The Laira airships were a common sight in Plymouth. The residents of the Cattewater villages would no doubt have had a good view of these inflated silver mobiles moving slowly overhead, departing or returning from their missions.

Sadly there were mishaps. Airship SS Z14 stationed at Chelson Meadow, while on a flight, developed engine failure and ballooned over the English Channel and landed in France in the trenches at Montreivil. Another airship attempting to land in a gusty wind at RNAS Laira became unmanageable, floated above the ground and came down in the Cattewater close to Mount Batten.

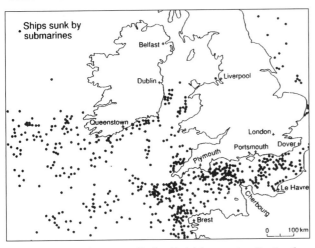

The U-boat offensive off the British coasts, September 1916–April 1917, showing the huge shipping losses by enemy submarines, particularly in the English Channel. (TAKEN FROM THE OFFICIAL HISTORY OF THE WAR.)

Men working on one of the smaller seaplane hangars that were being built in the area close to the Mount Batten Breakwater, c.1917.

The Birth of a Flying Boat Station

The Admiralty decided to introduce seaplanes or land planes for anti-submarine work. In addition, policy dictated that airships should be confined to reporting and keeping watch on U-boats and giving warnings to divert shipping. Aircraft, meanwhile, would be used as an offensive weapon. In South West England a search was made for suitable seaplane bases and it proved rather difficult to find sites offering the necessary shelter. Eventual two sites were acquired – one at Cattewater and the other at Newlyn. The seaplane station at Plymouth would be built on the headland of Mount Batten and named RNAS Cattewater. Prior to building the flying boat station Mount Batten was primarily a wide stretch of grassland, simply a very large uneven field, with pathways that ended up by the old quarry and the ancient round tower. Projecting out from the headland was the Mount Batten Breakwater. A flimsy wire fence marked the boundary, but was inadequate to prevent people from walking to the headland.

The decision to build a seaplane station on Mount Batten proved to be rather unpopular, particularly when it was discovered that local people would be denied their right of way across the land and prevented from using the seashore and its small sandy beach. The nearby golf course had already been closed because of the war. The minutes of the Oreston and Turnchapel Steamboat Company directors' meeting in February 1917 records that, 'as the Government has taken possession of the field and cottages the construction of a new pier at Mount Batten would be postponed'. Furthermore the local

The second of the small hangars being roofed, c.1917, with the repair shops by the side already completed. Between these hangars a slipway would later be constructed.

The Cattewater seaplane station in the making. Two completed airmen's huts can be seen. In the distance one of the large hangars, called a Type A shed by the Air Ministry, is being constructed. The bell tents (middle left) *are most likely temporary accommodation for the airmen. A date of 16 July 1917 is given on the original print.*

ferry would be prevented from landing passengers on the Mount Batten pier.

The building of the seaplane station commenced early in 1917 and went on throughout the rest of the war and during the early years of the aftermath. The last RNAS building was erected in 1922 – this continuation of building in peace time was evidence of the future plans of the RAF.

The newly established seaplane station covered 30 acres of land. As the ground had to be levelled, considerable amounts of earth and stone were removed using horse and carts. The two small hangars close to the breakwater and the airmen's huts near the coastguard cottages were the first to be erected. The coastguard cottages were converted as living quarters for married non-commissioned officers. The RNAS retained the Breakwater Inn along with the Castle Inn, the latter being renamed Green Leaf and was used as the official residence of the station's Commanding Officer for many years. The large hangars were built with their doors facing towards the Cattewater, away from the prevailing south-west winds that sweep across Plymouth Sound.

While this building work was proceeding in its early stages a Curtiss flying boat on transit arrived at Mount Batten. A rail track was laid along the Mount Batten Breakwater to enable a steam crane that originated from Devonport Dockyard, to move to and fro along the rails to hoist seaplanes in or out of the water. All this construction had changed Mount Batten beyond all recognition – it was no longer a rural retreat. Other than the hangars there were engineers' and carpenters' workshops, storerooms, a smithy and an annex for the important dope shop. Dope was a viscous solution and a volatile toxic chemical when inhaled. It was used for

strengthening the fabric of the aircraft and keeping them airtight.

RNAS Cattewater officially opened in April 1917 and the seaplane station became operational in August of the same year. There were nearly 600 RNAS personnel on the camp. As the submarine war against the enemy proceeded, the Admiralty's policy was to introduce land planes into the conflict as they were considered a more offensive weapon than seaplanes. A RNAS land station was opened at Prawle Point, some 7 miles from Kingsbridge. In the following summer a seaplane station under the command of RNAS Cattewater was opened at Torquay Harbour.

Early types of seaplanes were and looked delicate. When secured by buoys on the Cattewater, the aircraft, from a distance, looked like giant mosquitoes! If they did not arrive by air, they would be delivered to Turnchapel railway station where they would be taken to RNAS Cattewater and assembled. Soon after RNAS Cattewater was opened an American Curtiss H8 flying boat, having experienced engine failure, came down into the water outside Plymouth Sound and was towed back to Mount Batten.

During the summer and autumn of 1917 RNAS Cattewater was a place of considerable activity. In August the Admiralty issued a directive that outbound convoys of ships were to assemble in designated ports. In the South West, Falmouth and Plymouth were chosen, the faster ships reporting at Plymouth. Three convoys sailed from the port every seven days. Short 184 seaplanes were identified with Mount Batten. These were large aircraft at the time,

Left: *A panoramic view of Plymouth Hoe and part of RNAS Cattewater, c.1917, with the airmen's huts and aircraft on the breakwater together with the steam crane.*

Below: *The seaplane and kite-balloon station at Torquay Harbour that operated under the command of RAF Cattewater, c.1918.*

Right: *An interesting picture of one of the large hangars being built at Mount Batten. Through the steel girders a Curtiss flying boat can be seen out of the water. A glimpse of part of Turnchapel in the First World War can also be seen to the left of the picture.*

The cluster of newly built airmen's huts and the coast-guard cottages can be seen through the skeleton steel structures of the large hangar being built, c.1917.

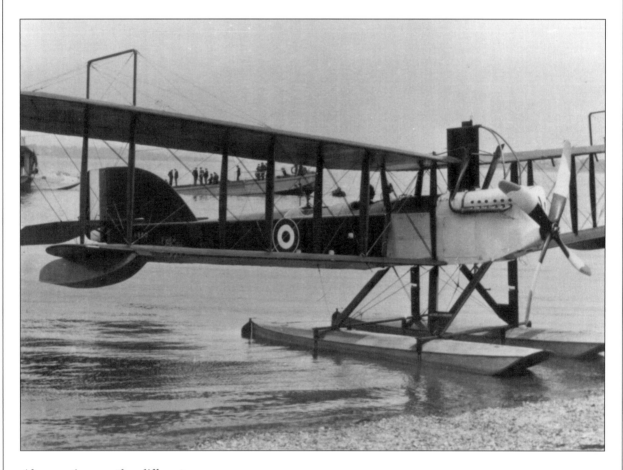

Above: *Among the different aircraft that were based at Mount Batten in 1917 were two Wight Converted seaplanes.*

An early photograph of Short 184 seaplanes on the breakwater. The rail track for the steam crane only extended halfway along the pier.

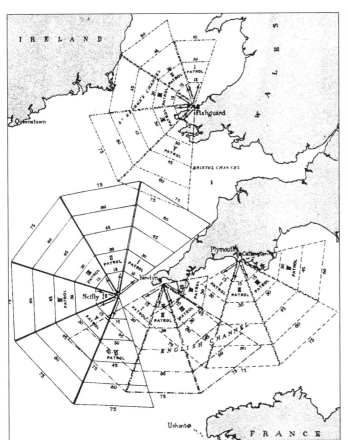

A chart taken from the official history of the Royal Air Force showing the system of seaplane and flying boat patrols from RNAS Cattewater in July 1917.

CATTEWATER (PLYMOUTH).

Marine Operations (Seaplane) Station, Nos. 237 and 238 Squadrons

(S.W. Area ; No. 9 (Operations) Group, 72nd Wing).

LOCATION.—England, Devonshire, ½ mile south-east of Plymouth, on the shores of Plymouth Sound.

Railway Stations :—Turnchapel (L. & S.W. Rly.), ¾ mile. Plymouth (L. & S.W. Rly.), 6 miles by road. Usual access by ferry or motor boat from Plymouth.

Road :—The roads are bad owing to steep hills.

Name :—This station is sometimes called " Mount Batten."

FUNCTION.—(a) Station for No. 237 Squadron, Headquarters and Nos. 420, 421, 422 and 423 (Float Seaplane) Flights for Anti-submarine Patrol duties. No. 238 Squadron, Headquarters and Nos. 347, 348 and 349 (Boat Seaplane, F. 3 type) for Anti-submarine Patrol duties. These Squadrons are under the control of the C.-in-C., Devonport, for Operations.

(b) This station is also used as a Store Base and Repair Depôt (Seaplanes) for No. 9 (Operations) Group.

ESTABLISHMENT.

Personnel.				Transport.			
Officers	..	..	84	Touring Cars ..	..	..	1
W.O.'s and N.C.O.'s above				Light Tenders	..	..	2
the rank of Corporal	..	34		Heavy Tenders	..	..	3
Corporals	..	..	32	Motor Cycles ..	..	..	5
Rank and File	..	..	348	Sidecars	..	..	3
Women	..	..	50	Ford ..	..	..	2
Women (Household)	..	35		Trailers	..	..	1
TOTAL (exclusive of Hostel Staff)			583	TOTAL	..	..	17
Machines.—Boat Seaplanes (F. 3 type)				..	..	..	9
	Float Seaplanes ..			..	..	..	24
				TOTAL	..	..	33

LAND.—The area occupied by this station is 30 acres, on a small peninsula almost surrounded by Plymouth Harbour. It is ½ mile by boat from Plymouth. The water is sheltered, with good mooring facilities. It stands about 15 feet above sea level.

TENURE POLICY.—Not at present on the list of permanent stations.

ACCOMMODATION.

Technical Buildings.	Map Reference.	Regimental Buildings.	Map Reference.
4 Seaplane Sheds—		Officers' Mess ..	3
Two, 200' × 100'	1	5 Officers' Quarters ..	—
Two, 180' × 60'	1	Officers' Baths ..	—
3 Slipways	—	Officers' Latrines ..	—
2 M.T. Sheds..	—	Sergeants' Mess (used as	
Workshops—		Women's Quarters) ..	—
Engineers', 123' × 20' (in		Sergeants' Latrines ..	—
annexe)	—	Sergeants' Baths ..	—
Carpenters', 80' × 33'	—	Regimental Institute	4
Dope, 40' × 20' (in		Regimental Store ..	—
annexe)	—	6 Men's Huts.. ..	—
Smiths' Shop	—	Men's Baths ..	—
4 General Stores	—	Men's Latrines and Ablu-	
3 Oil Stores ..	—	tion	—

An interesting official itemised document relating to RNAS Cattewater. The seaplane station had nearly 600 personnel on its establishment.

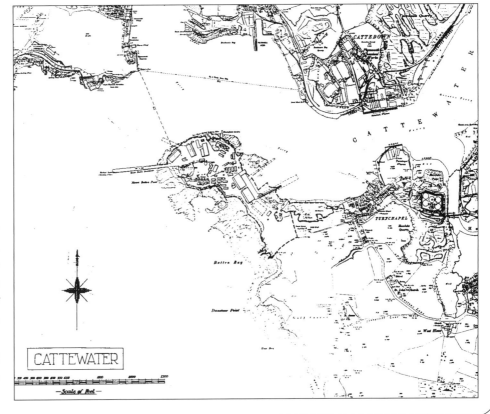

The layout of RNAS Cattewater showing the proposed plan to build another hangar and a new slipway. The golf course was close to the seaplane station. The Turnchapel oil tanks can be seen to the right of the map.

A classic picture of a row of Short 184 seaplanes on Mount Batten with the rail track laid near the end of the breakwater. At this time seaplanes were taken out of the water as soon as their flight had been completed to prevent water damage.

with a wing-span of 653 feet. Off they would go, loaded with bombs, on their patrols. On 28 August 1917, a Short 184 based at RNAS Cattewater attacked a U-boat off Bolt Head, but the bombs failed to explode.

When taken out of the sea, these aircraft would be stored in line on Mount Batten Breakwater, clearly visible from Plymouth Hoe. The Short 184 seaplanes at RAF Cattewater did sterling service on their anti-submarine duties, the pilots risking their lives, not always through enemy action but by being ditched into the sea because of the aircraft's engine failure. To put this into perspective, it is worth pointing out that there was no established air-sea rescue organisation, pilots did not, for some time, carry parachutes, but rather relied on the hope that if they had survived coming down in the water there would be by chance a ship nearby to rescue them. Between July and September six Mount Batten seaplanes crashed having suffered engine failure.

The aircrew at Mount Batten relied on the ground staff to service the aeroplanes' engines and to maintain the structure of the aircraft that were wooden framed. Even the floats were made of wood, which was easily damaged by water, so they required particular care. The fabric that covered the frame was easily torn, a ripped wing or tail-end could bring down a seaplane.

The RNAS Cattewater daily operational records include a bizarre report concerning a Short 184. A pilot on patrol thought at first he had sighted a U-boat off Prawle Point. It was in fact a whale breaking surface, but by the time the pilot realised his mistake he had dropped a bomb on the unfortunate creature hitting its tail.

There were many different aircraft at Mount Batten during the First World War, most of which were 'float planes', whose fuselage rested above the water, the floats giving the aircraft stability. In contrast to this, the hull body of flying boats rested in the water without sinking. The design of these aircraft were varied and fascinating.

During the winter of 1917 there were two Sopwith Baby tractor seaplanes based at RNAS Cattewater. Sir Thomas Sopwith (1888–1989), knighted in 1953 for his outstanding contribution to British aviation, was one of the truly great figures of the British aircraft industry. The Sopwith Camel, a Royal Flying Corps fighter biplane will forever be associated with the epic encounters that took place over the Western Front during the First World War. Sopwith Aviation Company (founded 1912) built early aircraft in what was once a skating-rink in Kingston, Surrey. He was certainly a man of vision. He went on to form the Hawker Siddeley Group in conjunction with Harry Hawker. In 1935 the company was involved in the design and build of the legendary Hawker Hurricane.

HMS Riviera, *a First World War seaplane carrier. Its duties included winching a seaplane out of the sea if it had suffered engine failure, assuming the aircraft was located, and delivering it back to its base. The* Riviera *was a familiar sight in Plymouth Sound.*

Left: The Short 184 seaplane is closely identified with Mount Batten in the First World War. This is an interesting picture taken at ground level showing activity on the breakwater. Aircraft N2799 was delivered to RNAS Cattewater in February 1918. There were variants of the 184, the one nearest the camera had four wooden propeller blades.

Right: A fine close-up picture of a twin-bladed Short 184 on the breakwater at RNAS Cattewater.

Left: A glimpse inside the workshop, or could this be a corner of a hangar at RNAS Cattewater? Tradesmen are repairing damaged seaplane floats.

Above: *A Sopwith Baby seaplane. Four of these aircraft arrived at RNAS Cattewater two months after the station opened.*

Left: *A rare photographic record of the original front of one of the large hangars that had recently been completed at Mount Batten during the First World War.*

This Sopwith Baby Tractor seaplane N1023, watched by nine airmen, arrived at RNAS Cattewater in May 1917, just two months after the station opened. N1023 attacked and bombed a German U-boat south of Land's End on 16 August 1917.

Above: *A Short 184 seaplane on patrol over the English Channel. The large ungainly floats of the aircraft resulted in it being referred to as 'Little Titch' after a popular music hall comedian of the time, who was small in stature and wore elongated boots on the stage as part of his act.*

Right: *The seaplanes in the First World War came in all shapes and sizes. The picture is of a Norman Thompson 4a Small America anti-submarine reconnaissance flying boat. Six of these aircraft were delivered to Mount Batten between the end of 1917 and the spring of 1918.*

Right: *One of the numerous wooden sheds at RNAS Cattewater was the station's Post Office. DSM Moseley calls to collect letters from the postman Jack Allen.*

The Aircraft Construction Company, a private concern, was responsible for building the Cattewater station. This rare picture shows a railway line alongside one of the smaller hangars. The rail is part of the breakwater line that a steam crane travelled along. A Short 184 seaplane and the tail end of another aircraft can be seen. The air station is still in the making as men are busy working on what will be the parade ground. Note the old-style sentry box.

Above: *On 1 April 1918 the ceremony of hauling down the white ensign on the transfer of the Royal Naval Air Service to the newly formed Royal Air Force took place outside the building that was once the Breakwater Inn. The flying boat station's name became RAF Cattewater.*

Right: *Among the various aircraft stationed at Mount Batten was the elegant Felixstowe F3. N4413 seen in the picture, taken c.1918, was attached to 347/8 flight of No. 238 Squadron. Nine Felixstowe F3 flying boats were based at RAF Cattewater.*

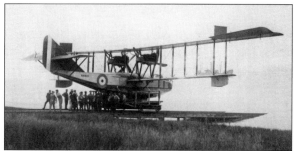

Inset, below: *A Curtiss 'Large America' patrol flying boat. Three of these aircraft had brief stays at the Cattewater in 1918.*

A close up of a Short Admiralty 184 Tractor seaplane N1768 with a two-man crew being lowered into the water off Mount Batten Breakwater. This aircraft was delivered in January 1918.

Above left: *Acting Lt Colonel F.K. Haskins, DSC, Officer Commanding RNAS/RAF Cattewater 1918. Haskins, once a Naval officer, was awarded the Distinguished Service Cross in 1916, when he was a pilot at Dunkirk participating in air raids on Ostend and Zeebrugge.*

Above, middle: *Lt Colonel P. Shepherd, Commanding Officer, in the aftermath period of the war. At this time officers were given Army rank titles. Shepherd was on active service in France from the early months of the war.*

Above right: *A happy picture of Corporal Farmer and Captain Hall at Mount Batten standing between the wooden propellers of a Felixstowe flying boat.*

Left: *Captain A.T. Sketchley (the rugby team captain) and Lt A.G. Hopkins, two popular officers at RAF Cattewater, c.1919.*

Sporting activities were an important part of service life at Mount Batten. The picture is interesting as it not only shows the members of the football team but indicates the type of uniforms worn by the airmen in the ranks. The fencing behind the men suggests it was taken at a racecourse, perhaps at Chelson Meadow.

This picture of the RAF Cattewater Rugby Team 1918–19, suggests there was still a number of airmen at Mount Batten in the immediate aftermath of the First World War.

Lt Colonel Shepherd with his officers photographed outside the officers' mess at Mount Batten, c.1919. The number of officers in Naval uniform was due to the period of transition from the Navy to the Air Force.

The country should forever more be indebted to Sopwith for when the Battle of Britain (August–October 1940) was fought he was able to supply aircraft, in addition to the Spitfire, that helped meet the challenge of the German Air Force. The Hawker Hurricane was the mainstay of the fighter force during those sterling times. A flight of these fighters was stationed at RAF Roborough during the Second World War for the defence of Plymouth.

If there were aircraft spotters in Plymouth in the First World War, for there were government charts printed to distinguish friendly aircraft from enemy ones, the spotters would have been spoilt for choice – not that there were enemy aircraft to be seen. There were, however, different types of seaplanes that were based on the Cattewater or were in transit. During

the winter of 1917 there were five Norman Thompson N.T. 4A small American flying boats based on the Cattewater to carry out anti-submarine reconnaissance.

An important change took place on 1 April 1918 when the Royal Naval Air Service and Royal Flying Corps were merged to create the Royal Air Force (RAF). The seaplane base at Mount Batten was at this time named RAF Cattewater. The occasion at Mount Batten was marked by a recommissioning ceremony held in front of the former Breakwater Inn. The station personnel were assembled and after a short speech the RAF flag was hoisted for the first time to replace the white ensign. Further changes occurred, including RAF Cattewater coming under the control of No. 19 Group, South West Area, and the

No more than a flimsy cover, but a copy of the front cover page of a souvenir publication extolling the important contribution made by the men who served at Mount Batten between 1917–19.

A picture of the ancient round tower taken during the First World War, at the time when the flying boat station was under construction.

Cattewater aircraft that were organised into flights were now formed into two new squadrons. During the summer months four Felixstowe F3 patrol flying boats were delivered to RAF Cattewater and were based there until January 1919.

Across the Cattewater, the towns of Devonport, Plymouth and Stonehouse had been united during 1914, and had been involved in so many ways with the progress of the war. The united towns were referred to as Fortress Plymouth. It was a place of military and Royal Marine barracks, so packed to capacity, some local schools became temporary barracks. Salisbury Road School became a military hospital as did Flete House located not far from the Cattewater villages. The Devonport naval base harboured the mighty warships of the Royal Navy. The vast Naval Dockyard was so busy that by the end of the war it had doubled the size of its workforce.

The war had come to the Cattewater – not only with the largest new development in the area, the flying boat base. In addition, friendly submarines sailed pass them to be refuelled at the Admiralty wharves situated behind the quarries. When America entered the war naval activity increased further; other than US warships arriving at Plymouth, a flotilla of United States Navy submarine chasers together with the destroyer USS *Aylwia* arrived and were based at the Victoria Wharves, Cattewater. The chasers had a radius of up to 1,200 miles and a maximum speed of 17 knots. Every boat had a radio telephone system installed enabling them to communicate from up to 20 miles away. Wireless technology was still in its infancy. The US naval officers were accommodated at Elliot Terrace on Plymouth Hoe close to the house of the Astors. Early in 1918 the largest contingent of the Women Royal Naval Service arrived at Plymouth and were accommodated in wooden huts at Mount Batten.

For the airmen who had no friends and relatives in or around Plymouth, there was not much choice in terms of entertainment. If they made their way to Plymouth they could visit the picture houses, which showed the silent films of Chaplin, or visit the local music halls. If the men ventured out of camp after church parade on a Sunday morning it would seem that the war was a world away as, except for people going to church, the streets were empty. The shops were closed and there was no outside entertainment. Public houses briefly opened at midday and in the evening, some men made their way to Hooe and Turnchapel. There are reports that some Mount Batten airmen attended the local church or chapels of Turnchapel and Oreston. RAF Cattewater did organise sports activities; the station had a very good rugby team that included officers and other ranks. It also had a soccer team.

When the war was over, most of the airmen were demobbed and the station's aircraft activities were run down. However, aircraft continued to visit or be based at Batten up until 1922. RAF Cattewater became a care and maintenance unit, no more than a place of deserted buildings. A large part of the flying boat station was left unattended allowing the weeds and wild bushes to thrive. However, the Air Ministry had, unknown to the local people, began to make plans for RAF Cattewater to become a permanent flying boat station.

This picture of HMS Rapid, *the official liberty boat for the airmen of RAF Cattewater, has been published many times. Research has revealed that it was taken on the morning of 11 November 1918 (Armistice Day).*

The United States Navy Curtiss flying boat NC4 after her epic transatlantic flight to Plymouth, arriving on 31 May 1919. The NC4 had been taken to Mount Batten for repair after hitting a buoy in Plymouth Sound.

The arrival of USN Curtiss NC4 attracted considerable attention throughout the country. The American crew were given a civic reception by Plymouth Town Council at the Mayflower Stone on 7 June 1919.

Chapter 3

Mount Batten Between the Wars

After the end of the First World War, RAF Cattewater was gradually run down as an operational base and the recently formed RAF squadrons associated with Mount Batten were disbanded. However there was still a presence of aircraft to be seen in the Cattewater, including Felixstowe flying boats based there until April 1921.

In August 1922 a Short Cromarty reconnaissance flying boat arrived at Mount Batten for a brief stay. These were aircraft whose appearance held a fascination for those who watched from Plymouth Hoe, but the aircraft that became the centre of attraction, not only at Plymouth but throughout the country, was the four-engine American Curtiss NC4 flying boat, flown by a crew of six, that touched down on the waters of Plymouth Sound on 31 May 1919, six months after the war had finished. The NC4 was one of three Curtiss flying boats that had originally set off on an epic flight to cross the Atlantic, but due to mishaps two of the aircraft were unable to complete the journey. Only the NC4 survived this first transatlantic crossing via Newfoundland and the Azores. The NC4 developed engine trouble on the flight from Lisbon to Plymouth and was forced down. The commander of the flying boat refused to risk landing at Plymouth during the night and stopped over at El Ferrol, Spain. The next day the Curtiss flying boat was escorted into Plymouth by three RAF Felixstowe F2A flying boats. As the NC4 was taxiing in Plymouth Sound it hit a buoy and was damaged.

This resulted in the flying boat being taken to RAF Cattewater to be repaired.

On 7 June, a week after arriving at Plymouth, the crew were given a civic reception at the Mayflower Stone on the Barbican. The American flying boats had not set out with the intention of being the first to fly non-stop across the Atlantic. This honour went, on 14 June 1919, to Captain John Alcock and Lieutenant Arthur Whitten Brown who flew for the first time across the ocean in a Vickers Vimy bomber from Newfoundland to Ireland. Both men were knighted after the flight.

Mount Batten had officially been reduced to a care and maintenance unit. What had been an operational flying boat station was now no more than a ghost station with a caretaker staff. The RAF was, unknown to the public, proposing to purchase the land at Mount Batten to continue its use as a seaplane station. The Imperial War Committee had, in these early postwar years, been reviewing the defence of the United Kingdom and had decided that the current theoretical enemy was France as it was at the time the only European country that possessed an air force capable of attacking Britain. As there were no air defences in the South West of England a decision was taken to reinforce the area by making Mount Batten an operational RAF station. It was argued there was no other suitable site in the region that could be used as a military airfield. The intention was also to reopen RAF Calshot that had been closed

A Felixstowe F2A flying boat N4570 being launched from the slipway at Mount Batten. Looking up the river there are two cable ships anchored in Clovelly Bay.

The N4570 inside one of the large Mount Batten hangars. The aircraft was based at RAF Cattewater between October 1920 and January 1921.

Pause for a rest after working on Felixstowe F2A, N4460 of No. 238 Squadron at Mount Batten. This flying boat suffered engine failure and force landed in the sea in January 1921.

A postcard dated 16 November 1920 of Mount Batten's seaplane station showing the wooden hutted accommodation that was used up to the 1930s, when it was replaced with brick buildings.

A painting by Edward Wadsworth of the Cattewater and Mount Batten, c.1923.

REPORT

FROM THE

SELECT COMMITTEE

ON THE

AIR MINISTRY (CATTEWATER SEAPLANE STATION) BILL.

TOGETHER WITH THE

PROCEEDINGS OF THE COMMITTEE AND MINUTES OF EVIDENCE.

Ordered, by the House of Commons, to be Printed.
17th July, 1925.

LONDON:
PRINTED & PUBLISHED BY HIS MAJESTY'S STATIONERY OFFICE.
To be purchased directly from H.M. STATIONERY OFFICE at the following addresses:
Adastral House, Kingsway, London, W.C.2; 28, Abingdon Street, London, S.W.1;
York Street, Manchester; 1, St. Andrew's Crescent, Cardiff;
or 120, George Street, Edinburgh;
or through any Bookseller.
1925
Price 3d. net.

Front cover of the Select Committee's Cattewater Seaplane Station Bill report, c.1925.

A peaceful scene at RAF Cattewater, before it was officially reopened. Although the station appears deserted there are three flying boats moored in the Cattewater.

The original officers' mess at Mount Batten. Compare this with the large brick building erected in the 1930s. In front of the entrance to the mess, two officers are sitting by two bombs displayed as a form of military decoration. The mess overlooked the Cattewater.

down after the war. Calshot was, however, planned to be used solely as a base for training.

During the First World War Mount Batten had been appropriated by the Admiralty under the Defence of the Realm Act. This was something of a draconian wartime act that meant the suspension of civil rights and allowed the Government to take over the land, (but not the ownership of it). Recently discovered files at the National Archives reveal that within seven months of the end of the First World War, the Air Council's intention was to purchase Mount Batten and use it as a permanent flying boat station. The Air Ministry showed its intentions by holding the 'Cattewater Conference' at Mount Batten on 14 June 1919 to discuss, among other things, the questions of the boundary sites. Another subject discussed included the building of an additional large hangar and slipway in the area where the officers' tennis-courts and disused mine were located. Various properties in the area, such as Mount Edgcumbe Villa in Turnchapel, were listed for the Air Ministry to hire. The purchase of Mount Batten was not to exceed £30,000.

Among the numerous problems associated with the Government purchasing Mount Batten was its failure to reach a financial settlement with some of the interested parties. An extension to negotiate had been granted, but as no agreement was forthcoming, the Air Council submitted a notice to acquire the land by a compulsory order that the court granted. It took until 1925 for The Cattewater Seaplane Bill to be presented in Parliament by the Under Secretary of State for Air, Sir Philip Sassoon. The Cattewater Commissioners and freeholders of the land were compensated, certain rights were reserved for the Duchy of Cornwall and the Earl of Morley, the latter claiming his interests

amounted to £24,000, while Plymouth's Octagon brewery settled for £1,700 for the Castle Inn, cottage, boathouse and 18 acres of land and gardens that had been leased from the Earl of Morley for a period of 30 years. At arbitration someone had the foresight to draw attention to the potential of the land at Mount Batten for industrial and leisure development. On 12 August 1925 the House of Lords agreed to the bill and two days later it was given royal assent. However, the public were indignant as they were still banned from areas of land they previously had access to – in fact, all the public rights of way at Mount Batten were now legally taken from them. Public landing on Batten's foreshore was forbidden, resulting in the Oreston and Turnchapel Steamboat Company claiming substantial amounts of money for the loss of income.

The immediate task of the RAF once the station had been acquired by the Ministry was to refurbish the camp. This included clearing the undergrowth of bramble and weeds. A near disaster occurred when one of the four bombs, each bomb painted red, white and blue that had stood outside the officers' mess since the First World War, exploded as it was being removed. No one was injured but considerable damage was done to the nearby buildings. A Court of Enquiry was convened, resulting in the Air Ministry issuing an order that all bombs used for display purposes at RAF establishments must be inspected and if necessary made safe.

After the undergrowth was cleared additional paths and roads were laid. Part of the Cattewater was dredged to construct a new enlarged slipway in front of the two large hangars in anticipation of the new flying boats that would be based at RAF Cattewater.

Lawns were set out to give the station an orderly appearance, but Mount Batten still retained the overall appearance of a community of wooden huts, much the same as it did during the First World War.

In the years following the war military aircraft continued to be constructed based on wartime designs, but as the decade of the 1920s progressed a new generation of aircraft constructed of metal frames (to replace the traditional wooden frames), were being introduced. This change did not happen overnight; the RAF still preferred biplanes to monoplanes. Although technically wanting and slow compared with the high performances of aircraft of the twenty-first century, the aeroplanes of the 1920s and 1930s reflected significant advances in performance. There was, in spite of the poor international economic situation, plenty of aeronautical development and competition among nations. The peace treaty that followed the First World War prevented Germany from manufacturing military aircraft. In the 1920s Germany built gliders and used them to train the future pilots of the German Air Force that during the 1930s would supply the crews of Hitler's newly created Luftwaffe, that had secretly been built.

Mount Batten became recognised between the wars as a place from which long-distance pioneering flights started. The first of these flights was by two RAF Supermarine Southampton flying boats that left RAF Cattewater on 1 July 1926 for Egypt and Cyprus and returned to Plymouth during the first week of August. The Commanding Officer in charge of RAF Cattewater at this time was Flight Lieutenant E.V. Andrewertha, who would leave to take up a post at RAF Northolt. He was replaced by Flight Lieutenant A.J. Redman, a junior officer who, according to Air Vice Marshall Cracroft, was sent to open the station. During this period commercial flying boat companies and the Royal Air Force were continuing to identify and establish suitable bases in different parts of the British Empire.

An outstanding British pioneering flying achievement at this time was the 23,000-mile cruise undertaken by four Southampton flying boats commanded by Group Captain Cave-Brown-Cave. The crews flew from Plymouth in October 1927, travelling to Singapore, around the Australian continent and on to Japan before returning to their base at Singapore. Limits of performance compared to contemporary flight endurance are reflected by the fact that the aircraft had to alight 29 times for refuelling between England and Singapore.

A Southampton flying boat No. S1301 of No. 203 Squadron pictured against Plymouth Hoe, making for its mooring in the Cattewater, c.1929.

RAF Cattewater Reopens

Ten years after the end of the First World War, RAF Cattewater was officially reopened on 22 August 1928. There was an increased complement of 140 airmen in anticipation of the arrival of additional flying boats that were to be delivered by the end of the year. Within a month of RAF Cattewater reopening a Blackburn Iris, the latest type of flying boat coming in to service for the RAF, arrived at the station to take Sir Philip Sassoon, the Under Secretary of State for Air, on an extended cruise to the Middle East, Iraq and India to evaluate the Blackburn's capabilities under varying climatic conditions. Sir Philip departed from the Cattewater on 26 September 1928 and returned to England on 14 November. There were nine people in the plane, one of them being Sassoon's valet who became air sick. This meant the Under Secretary had to look after him.

In January 1929 RAF Cattewater went operational when No. 203 Squadron was formed from No. 482 (General Reconnaissance) Flight. No. 203 (flying boat) Squadron was equipped with twin-engine Supermarine Southamptons, a relative new aircraft designed by R.J. Mitchell of Spitfire fame. This new squadron was soon to leave Mount Batten for service in Iraq.

In 1929 RAF Cattewater had a new Commanding Officer, Wing Commander Sydney Smith, OBE, who had served in the Middle East during the early 1920s, then at the RAF College at Cranwell. He arrived at Mount Batten from the Air Ministry, having been appointed to organise the 1929 Schneider Trophy event to be held at RAF Calshot. The races were to take place above the waters of Spithead (the eastern

Above: *Wing Commander Sydney Smith* (fourth from the right), *Commanding Officer of RAF Mount Batten, 1928–31.*

Left: *Visitors queuing up to examine a flying boat in a hangar at Mount Batten, c.1929, on the occasion of the first 'At Home' allowing members of the public to visit the station. It shows the women's fashion of the time.*

A Fairey 111D seaplane attached to No. 204 Squadron formed in 1929 at RAF Cattewater.

Non-commissioned Officers of No. 209(FB) Squadron at Mount Batten in 1930. The back row includes: *Cpl Prestidge, Sgt Marsh, Cpl Martin, Sgt Saffety, Sgt Hunter, Cpl Lawry;* left to right, middle row: *Flight Officer Bonsey (Adj), Squadron Leader Jones (Co), Flight Sergeant Hughes;* sitting, front: *Cpl Petch, Cpl Hine, Cpl Jon. The men in the front row have not been identified.*

part of the Channel between the mainland and the Isle of Wight). Sydney Smith, called 'Smudger Smith' by his rankers, was a popular Commanding Officer. His official residence at Mount Batten was the old Castle Inn, where he lived with his wife and daughter.

At the time Wing Commander Sydney Smith was busy at Mount Batten organising the 1929 Schneider Trophy races, few people were aware of the considerable amount of planning that was carried out at RAF Cattewater for this prestigious event. Sydney Smith flew the Prince of Wales (later the Duke of Windsor) around the Schneider Trophy course. In February Mount Batten became more active as No. 204 Squadron was re-formed, equipped with Fairey 111 seaplanes and later Southampton flying boats.

In February 1929 the legendary Lawrence of Arabia reported for duty at RAF Cattewater under the name of Aircraftman T.E. Shaw. He was to stay at Mount Batten for four years and while there he established links with Hooe and Turnchapel. Security at the RAF station was lapse up until Lawrence arrived; visitors had no problem in entering the base to meet friends and relations. All changed when he arrived – official passes were now required when the young women attended the station dance on a Saturday evening. A separate chapter describing the life of Lawrence (Shaw) while at Mount Batten is the subject of the next chapter.

On his arrival Lawrence soon became aware that the flying boat base was a place of contentment. The seaplane station was known as 'Lady Astor's camp'. As one of the Members of Parliament for Plymouth Lady Astor used her influence to grant a concession for West Country airmen to be stationed near their homes. A third of the men serving on the station lived in the district of Plymouth. By submitting an application to the commanding officer they were granted a sleeping-out pass, unique at the time in the Royal Air Force. When the day's duties were finished at 4p.m. the men collected their pass and made their exit en masse from the camp. Some took the long walk from Mount Batten down the narrow road through Turnchapel to take the ferry across to Plymouth. Alternatively they went to the station to catch the local train. An additional ferry service was provided by Bill Dunne, a local licensed boat owner. Dunne ran a water-taxi service from the Plymouth Barbican. He had permission to bring his boat alongside the Mount Batten Breakwater to collect the airmen passengers. The following morning Dunne would be waiting at the Barbican to take them back to Mount Batten for the first morning parade. Dunne charged a few extra pence for this convenience that the men thought was worth it, as any man absent or late on parade without permission could end up having his pass withdrawn.

Officers of No. 209 Squadron that was formed in January 1929. The Squadron was equipped with Blackburn Iris flying boats. Seated in the centre of the front row is Squadron Leader Jones.

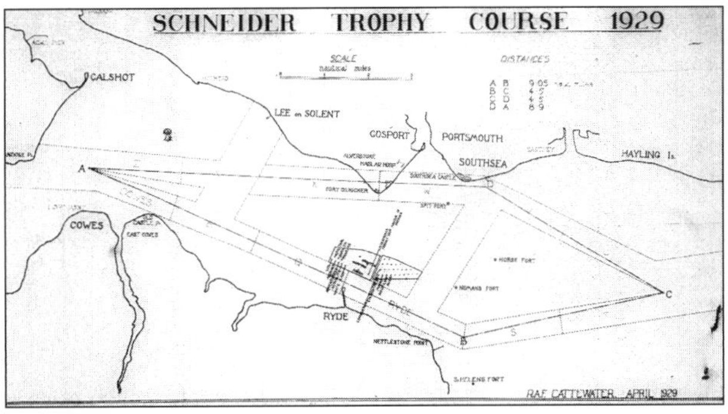

Considerable planning for the Schneider Trophy event was carried out at Mount Batten, as shown by this plan of the course that was produced at RAF Cattewater.

The year 1929 was when Mount Batten held the first of many open days, that fell on Empire Day. The event allowed the public into the seaplane station – until then local people had no ideas what was going on there. Open day was partly a colourful fête with visiting officers from all the services in their dress uniforms, embellished with gold braid and red sashes mixing with the crowd. A hangar would be decorated with flags. Visitors could sit down and be served with refreshments as a band played popular music. There were sporting events for the airmen with Lady Astor donating the prizes. People queued to see inside the aircraft and watched the flying displays with excitement.

As there was no resident RAF Medical Officer at the camp, Dr Noye Scott, the well-known local village doctor took the station's sick parade. Men with minor ailments were treated at the camp's sick bay. Serious clinical conditions and dental treatment were referred to the Royal Naval Hospital, Devonport.

The airmen were billeted in hutted accommodation built in 1917. The nearby terrace of coastguard cottages that faced out to the Plymouth Sound were still used to accommodate the non-commissioned officers, while the senior officers lived in substantial buildings on the edge of the camp. The airmen's mess was in another wooden hut. The camp food was acknowledged to be good for one reason: Clare Smith, the wife of the commanding officer was on the canteen committee and suggested for a small weekly voluntary donation by the airmen, a more interesting menu could be supplied. This meant the serving of an occasional roast beef dinner or a breakfast of fried bacon and eggs.

Sunday church parade was compulsory at the camp. The church was a wooden hut so small that it meant a rota was prepared for the men to attend morning service. At this period the station's church stood facing east across Plymouth Sound. Several airmen recalled that in order to relieve the boredom of the sermon, they would look out of the window across the Sound and count the number of portholes of the passenger ships that were at anchor. In the 1930s Plymouth was an important port of call for ocean-going liners. Many American passengers on their grand European tour would disembark and take a train from Millbay Station (Plymouth) to London to give them an extra day in England, rather than wait for their ship to dock further up the English Channel.

At Hooe and Turnchapel airmen would be seen walking through the villages dressed in their thick blue serge uniform. The jacket was required to be buttoned up to the neck, not open as it is now, one of the reforms suggested by Lawrence when he was stationed at Mount Batten. The men wore a peak cap. If out on a pass they were compelled to carry a silver-topped swagger cane, to convey an image of discipline and smartness. In the early 1930s tennis-courts and squash courts for the ranks were set out and a gymnasium was constructed.

In January 1930, No. 209 Squadron was re-formed at RAF Mount Batten consisting of three Blackburn Iris flying boats. During this year a pioneering flight of three Southampton flying boats of No. 204 Squadron departed from Plymouth to participate in the Icelandic Parliament celebrations, but with the purpose of setting up the longest distance formation flight. On this historic flight Wing Commander Sydney Smith developed appendicitis and his aircraft was diverted to the Faroes where he was taken to hospital.

Flying boats, as with land planes, were getting larger, the more powerful engines leading to an increase in performance in terms of speed and flying distance. The seaplanes were tethered to buoys in the calmer

A Supermarine Southampton with beaching gear. The image shows the contemporary scene across the Cattewater in 1930. To the right of the gracious fishing boat, is a small steam ferry making for Oreston and Turnchapel.

Across the water from Mount Batten in the early 1930s was the busy Barbican Fish Market in Plymouth. The picture shows the East Coast Herring Fleet tied up alongside the quayside.

waters of the Cattewater. To take off and descend they used a designated stretch of water in Plymouth Sound. Whenever a Cattewater flying boat began its ascent or touched down it was accompanied at a distance by an RAF launch as a safety precaution. Occasionally there was an accident; one Cattewater aircraft came down into the sea out in the English Channel but the station's RAF launches were unable to travel beyond the break-water. Clare Smith, wife of the commanding officer recorded being at Mount Batten and watching a float fall away from a seaplane when it was flying in the air.

A Changing City

Although Plymouth had recently been designated a city, except for the honour this brought, none of the citizens really benefited. The city in the early 1930s was a vibrant regional shopping centre. This was a period of social revolution with the beginning of mass entertainment. Plymouth was rapidly becoming a cinema-going city as the recent introduction of talking pictures had brought about the opening of the first luxury picture houses. Crowds sometimes up to 30,000 went to see Plymouth Argyle and the young people broke convention to meet up with the opposite sex, without first having to be introduced, by crowding the dance halls to quickstep and foxtrot.

Tragedy Strikes

On 4 February 1931 there was a tragic event involving an Iris flying boat from No. 209 Squadron that was on Air Defence exercises, co-operating with fighter aircraft stationed at Roborough airfield. Blackburn Iris flying boats flew with a crew of nine but on the day of the disaster an Iris (S 238) took off from Plymouth Sound carrying 12 officers and other ranks to carry out firing practice. After an hour's practice the S 238 began its descent to touch down on the water. To the surprise and horror of those on the land watching the aircraft, instead of straightening out, the S 238 nosedived into the water of the Sound, creating a loud booming noise. People in the city's shopping centre thought an explosion had occurred somewhere in Plymouth. An observer recorded that the impact of the aircraft striking the water produced a wall of large waves that closed down on the doomed flying boat. After a momentary pause one of the aircraft's floats surfaced, followed by the tip of the rudder. Wilfred Little, a Plymouth Harbour pilot and Harry Hole who were out sailing in the Sound were first at the scene of the incident and rescued two men who were clinging to the wreckage. Wing Commander Smith and T.E. Lawrence, the latter having seen the flying boat crash into the water, arrived in one of the station's launches and rescued two other airmen. Wing Commander Smith allowed Lawrence to take charge in the search for survivors, but all hope of saving anyone else alive had gone. On hearing the news people of the city made for Plymouth Hoe and the cliff tops at Bovisand. This was the first fatal accident that had occurred since the station had become operational three years previously. Of the four airmen rescued one died from his injuries.

The formal enquiry to identify the victims of the crash was held at the Royal Naval Hospital,

Above: *A Blackburn Iris flying boat being serviced in one of the large hangars at Mount Batten. No. 209 Squadron was equipped with three of these aircraft.*

Right: *The R100 airship photographed from Mount Batten, moving towards Plymouth. The R100 was the sister ship to the ill-fated R101 that was destroyed on its maiden flight with a great loss of life.*

A Blackburn Iris 111 in flight over the South Devon coast. It was one of these aircraft that was involved in the flying boat disaster in Plymouth Sound during February 1931.

Salvaging the floats of the Blackburn Iris flying boat after it crashed into the waters of Plymouth Sound in February 1931.

The flying disaster in Plymouth Sound when nine lives were lost when a Blackburn Iris flying boat nosedived into the water in February 1931. Crowds of people stood on the cliffs at Jennycliff watching the disaster.

Stonehouse, but six airmen were still missing. Plymouth's Guildhall was used for the Court of Enquiry but the public were forbidden to attend. The court's finding, regarding the cause of the disaster, was that a wing commander had pulled rank on a junior pilot by taking over the controls of S 238; this action resulting in the wing commander crashing the flying boat into the water. It was revealed that the wing commander, although a qualified pilot, was not proficient in piloting flying boats. Reports had been submitted to the Air Ministry regarding the officer being unfit to pilot flying boats but no decisive had been taken to act on these reports. The outcome of the Court of Enquiry was that an order was issued that stated when an aircraft was in flight, the pilot, whatever his rank, was in charge of the aircraft. Other than blaming the wing commander

who had lost his life, no-one else was incriminated. No-one, as far as it is known, was dismissed, demoted or reprimanded.

On the day of the funeral for the victims of the disaster, thousands of people lined the streets of

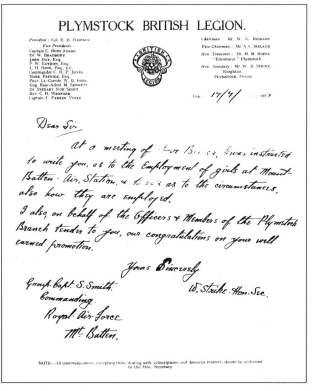

A letter dated 17 July 1931 to the Commanding Officer of Mount Batten from the local British Legion querying the employment of civilian girls at the air station. In reply to the letter the Commanding Officer of RAF Mount Batten explains the girls employed at Mount Batten are from the Blackburn Aeroplane Company, Hull, the constructors of the Iris flying boats.

Supermarine Southampton No. S1232 based at RAF Mount Batten developed engine problems while flying off the North Cornwall coast and came down in the sea. The flying boat was towed into Padstow Harbour where it was repaired and flown back to Plymouth, May 1931.

Plymouth to pay their respects to the dead. It was a sad but impressive procession that started outside the Royal Naval Hospital, Stonehouse. The gun carriage bearing the coffin of the ill-fated wing commander was diverted on route and proceeded to Plymouth North Road Station, where the body was taken to Loughborough for burial. The main funeral procession proceeded to Ford Park Cemetery. As it was impossible to accommodate all the mourners in the chapel, the burial service was held by the grave-side with a special service held in Plymouth Sound over the water where the flying boat crashed.

T.E. Lawrence, who had attended the Court of Enquiry, took the opportunity to request that the RAF upgrade its obsolete launches and replace them with power crafts that could be used as rescue boats. Such a boat had been designed and built by Hubert Scott-Paine. The prototype, RAF 200, after satisfactory completion of preliminary trials at Stokes Bay, Dorset, was taken to Mount Batten, where Lawrence was chosen as one of the crew members to participate in extended trials of the launch.

Accidents continued to happen. For example, a Supermarine Southampton of No. 204 Squadron flying along the North Cornish coast developed engine trouble and came down in the sea. The seaplane was towed into Padstow Harbour where it attracted considerable attention. Mechanics arrived from RAF Mount Batten to repair the engine before it was flown back to Plymouth.

Activities in the Air: the Mid–Late 1930s

There was another royal flight on 6 June 1931 in a Mount Batten aircraft when Wing Commander Sydney Smith piloting a Southampton flying boat flew Prince George (later King George VI) to Dartmouth.

Two years after the 1931 flying boat disaster in Plymouth Sound, another Blackburn Iris flying boat was involved in an accident. As three of these Mount Batten aircraft were circling in the sky another Blackburn Iris was having difficulty becoming airborne. The aircraft eventually gathered speed to take off from the water but continued straight ahead towards a Naval launch, which it struck with its wing. The flying boat turned over and sunk. One person was killed and three others were injured. The memory of the 1931 disaster was in everyone's mind. The formal inquest was held at the Jubilee Hall in Turnchapel. The official inquiry held at Mount

A Blackburn Perth, K3581 of No. 209 Squadron on the Cattewater, c.1934.

Batten published a brief statement that engine failure was the cause of the crash. T.E. Lawrence, who had gone out to the scene of the crash, was critical of the salvage operation and submitted proposals on how the procedure could be improved.

The Blackburn Iris flying boats remained at Mount Batten until 1 May 1935 when No. 209 Squadron was re-equipped with Blackburn Perths – larger and more powerful machines. In 1935 No. 209 Squadron transferred to Felixstowe.

Mount Batten was home to a small marine dock known at the time as Sydney's Folly, a reference to Wing Commander Sydney Smith, who had been responsible for building it.

The Southamptons of No. 204 Squadron were replaced with Supermarine Scapas in August 1935. In April 1935 the strength of the station was 20 officers and 185 airmen. Six months later this was reduced to 96 airmen and six officers.

There was yet more aircraft movement at Mount Batten during 1935 when Hawker Ospreys and 111Fs were stationed there. These Flights were based at Mount Batten for two years, before returning to the Fleet Air Arm base, Lee-on-Solent, in November 1937.

During 1936 a notable flight was made from RAF Mount Batten to Singapore to evaluate the trans-India flight route during the monsoon season. This turned out to be a difficult and dangerous experience for those involved. In October No. 204 Squadron set out on a ten-month detachment in the Mediterranean to be based at Alexandra its before return to Plymouth. The following year No. 204 Squadron was equipped with another new flying boat, the Saro London, and the squadron was ordered to Malta for naval exercises. After a visit to Australia to represent the Royal Air Force at the 150th anniversary celebrations of Sydney University No. 204 Squadron

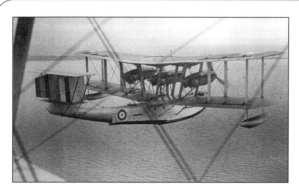

Blackburn Iris 111, S1263 that was involved in a fatal accident at Plymouth Sound on 12 January 1933, when engine failure prevented the flying boat from becoming airborne.

Above: *This small marine craft harbour was built in the early 1930s. It was named 'Sydney's Folly' after Wing Commander Sydney Smith.*

Above: *The tranquil setting of a Supermarine Southampton seen against the Castle Inn and ancient round tower.*

On the greens of the United Services Golf Course, overlooking RAF Mount Batten. It was here that the pioneer aviator Amy Johnson landed in a Moth aircraft to be greeted by Lawrence of Arabia.

Crew boarding one of the two Perth flying boats at the Cattewater that was to fly to Greenland in September 1934, in order to survey the land as a possible northern flying route to America.

A Saro London 1 K5263 of No. 204 Squadron, c.1935.

Right: *Visitors to the base on Empire Air Day 1935 follow the launching of a Supermarine Walrus down a slipway at Mount Batten. The Walrus was known as a pusher aircraft with its propeller fixed at the rear of the wing structures.*

A Westland Wapiti 11A attached to No. 444 Fleet Fighter Flight taxiing on the Cattewater opposite the Royal Citadel, Plymouth, c.1932. The Wapiti was a fighter aircraft but three of them were fitted with floats as an experiment. On the extreme right of the picture is a black hole in the sloping wall. People coming off the ferry at Phoenix Wharf making for Plymouth Hoe would walk up the steps and go through the tunnel. Later Madeira Road was extended to allow access to the Barbican.

Above: *A gracious aerial picture of a Saro London in flight over Plymouth.*

Right: *Accidents happen, as was the fate of the Saro London K5910 that caught fire in the Cattewater on 31 March 1937.*

Left: *Details of the daily routine of an aircraftman at RAF Mount Batten and the type of food he was served during the 1930s. This was a handout given to the public on an open day at the station.*

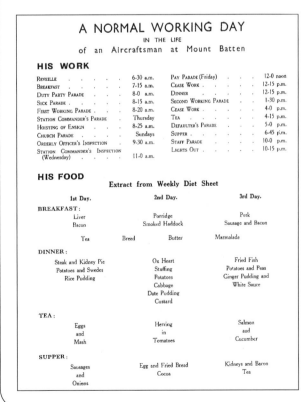

A NORMAL WORKING DAY
IN THE LIFE
of an Aircraftsman at Mount Batten

HIS WORK

Reveille	6-30 a.m.	Pay Parade (Friday)	12-0 noon
Breakfast	7-15 a.m.	Cease Work	12-15 p.m.
Duty Party Parade	8-0 a.m.	Dinner	12-15 p.m.
Sick Parade	8-15 a.m.	Second Working Parade	1-30 p.m.
First Working Parade	8-20 a.m.	Cease Work	4-0 p.m.
Station Commander's Parade	Thursday	Tea	4-15 p.m.
Hoisting of Ensign	8-25 a.m.	Defaulter's Parade	5-0 p.m.
Church Parade	Sundays	Supper	6-45 p.m.
Orderly Officer's Inspection	9-30 a.m.	Staff Parade	10-0 p.m.
Station Commander's Inspection (Wednesday)	11-0 a.m.	Lights Out	10-15 p.m.

HIS FOOD

Extract from Weekly Diet Sheet

	1st Day.	2nd Day.	3rd Day.
BREAKFAST:	Liver	Porridge	Pork
	Bacon	Smoked Haddock	Sausage and Bacon
	Tea	Bread	Butter	Marmalade
DINNER:	Steak and Kidney Pie	Ox Heart	Fried Fish
	Potatoes and Swedes	Stuffing	Potatoes and Peas
	Rice Pudding	Potatoes	Ginger Pudding and
		Cabbage	White Sauce
		Date Pudding	
		Custard	
TEA:	Eggs	Herring	Salmon
	and	in	and
	Mash	Tomatoes	Cucumber
SUPPER:	Sausages	Egg and Fried Bread	Kidneys and Bacon
	and	Cocoa	Tea
	Oniens		

During the 1930s flying boats were getting larger and more powerful. The RAF was, however, still using biplanes. This picture is of a Short Singapore moored at Mount Batten in May 1937.

Above: *A Fairey 111F seaplane with floats almost as long as its fuselage flying low above the Cattewater, c.1937. These were Royal Navy reconnaissance aircraft attached to capital ships of the Home Fleet.*

Right: *A Fairey Swordfish float plane on the concourse, in front of the hangars at Mount Batten on Empire Day, 25 June 1935.*

A Hawker Osprey K3649 being serviced in one of the Mount Batten hangars.

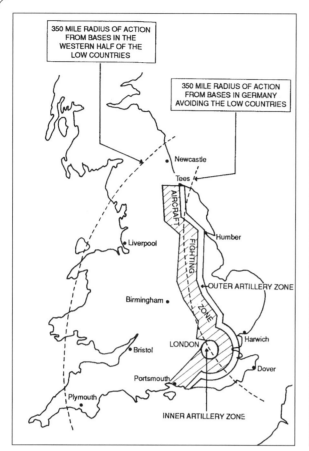

The reorientation scheme, 1935, for the air defence of Great Britain against the possibility of attack by the German Airforce. This official scheme was based on the belief that air attacks would be directed against London and the eastern side of England. Until the outbreak of the Second World War RAF Mount Batten was the only operational base in South West England.

Top: *On the site of the RAF officers' mess there is now a terrace of houses that stand alone, the fronts facing out to Plymouth Sound.*

Above: *A Short Rangoon S1435 on the Cattewater, perhaps in transit and not based at Mount Batten.*

Across the water from Mount Batten, the shopping centre of Plymouth in the 1930s became vibrant on Saturdays as people arrived from all over the South West.

ROYAL AIR FORCE STATION, MOUNT BATTEN, PLYMOUTH.

Programme of

FLYING EVENTS
and
GROUND DISPLAYS

WEDNESDAY, 25th MAY, 1938
and
SATURDAY, 28th MAY 1938.

TIME TABLE OF FLYING EVENTS

Event—

1.	1400—1430 hrs. (2—2.30 p.m.)	A "Walrus" amphibian flying boat will go down the slipway, take off, land and return up the slipway.
2.	1430—1500 hrs. (2.30—3 p.m.)	Dive bombing attack on a motor boat by three "Osprey" two-seater fighters.
3.	1505—1530 hrs. (3.5—3.30 p.m.)	Flight Aerobatics by three "Fury" single-seater fighter.
4.	1530—1600 hrs. (3.30—4 p.m.)	Low flying attack against ground forces by "Swordfish" three-seater seaplane.
5.	1600—1630 hrs. (4—4.30 p.m.)	A demonstration of bombing practice over the Camera Obscura by a 'London' Flying Boat.
6.	1630—1700 hrs. (4.30—5 p.m.)	Individual Aerobatics by a "Fury" single-seater fighters.
7.	1700—1730 hrs. (5—5.30 p.m.)	A demonstration of taking off and landing by a "London" Flying Boat.
8.	1730—1800 hrs. (5.30—6 p.m.)	An attack on a "Swordfish" seaplane by three "Osprey" fighters.
9.	1800—	A formation fly-past by the aircraft taking part in the display.

Whereas Devonport Naval base had its Navy days, the Royal Air Force had an annual open day at Mount Batten when the public would come to inspect the flying boats and watch the spectacular flying displays.

A timetable of flying events in 1938 in which various aircraft took part in the display.

The terraced houses were the married quarters for the airmen serving at RAF Mount Batten. The photographer would have been standing in the vicinity of where St Luke's Hospice stands in 2006.

A Fairey 111F seaplane on the slipway at Mount Batten. Two flights of these Fleet Air Arm reconnaissance aircraft arrived at the flying boat station in May 1935. In the distant background is a view of Turnchapel ferry pier.

returned to Plymouth and started to prepare for war.

RAF Mount Batten continued to hold its open day and air show on Empire Day; the event continued to attract crowds of people. In 1937, 2,800 people visited the station and watched the fly-pasts of the latest aircraft. One aircraft that flew around Plymouth was the new Hawker Hurricane, a monoplane, watched by spectators who at the time could not have envisaged the important part this new plane would play in their lives in the coming war. The public on Plymouth Hoe were fascinated by the silver-painted flying boats that gracefully descended onto the surface of the water, producing spray like a flying fish. There must have been observers who looked across Plymouth Sound and wished they could be in one of these graceful aircraft and fly away, beyond the blue horizon.

The political crisis was worsening; war threatened. The RAF had realised their recent flying boat the Saro London would be outclassed if there was a war, so for this reason No. 204 Squadron waited for the delivery of the Short Sunderland flying boats, a military aircraft completely different from previous RAF flying boats, for it was a monoplane and, for its time, a giant of an aircraft.

The mid-1930s had seen a significant change in Mount Batten when the reconstruction program took place. Many of the original wooden structures were demolished and replaced with purpose-built brick buildings, giving a barracks look about the place. The aircraft hangars, stores and workshops, although they retained their appearance, were reclad. A new officers' mess designed in the neo-Georgian style was built to look out across Plymouth Sound. This building has, in recent years, been demolished and replaced with a small row of terraced houses. The tempo of aircraft movement was increased. No. 821 Squadron of the Fleet Air Arm was based at Mount Batten for a short time. No. 2 Anti-Aircraft Co-operation units of Blackburn Sharks arrived but eventually moved in the early period of the war to RAF St Eval. The Sharks were mainly used for target towing, to provide firing practice for the Royal Gunnery School at Devonport.

In September 1938, the crisis leading to the Munich Agreement, that threatened war, resulted in RAF Mount Batten receiving orders for its defences to be put into operation. The ancient tower was covered in camouflage paint. A contingent of 61 airmen of the RAF Volunteer Reserve reported to Mount Batten. In addition, officers and 60 men of the Middlesex Regiment TA had arrived to take up the defence of the station against sabotage. Two days before war was declared the armourers were preparing bombs to be used by the flying boats for immediate use. The seaplane station was to see wartime action again.

Chapter 4

Aircraftman T.E. Shaw (Lawrence of Arabia)

A Hero At Mount Batten

An important aspect of the history of Mount Batten is the presence of Lawrence of Arabia who served at the RAF station between 1929 and 1932 under the name of Aircraftman T.E. Shaw. In 1927 he had changed his birth name by deed poll to Shaw so as to avoid unwanted attention, but in this text he will be referred to as Lawrence. His years at Mount Batten are very interesting as he pursued an active social life, about which, until recently, relatively little was known. While stationed at Mount Batten he advocated the need for the RAF to introduce air-sea rescue.

Lawrence was born in Tramadoc, North Wales and was christened Thomas Edward. He was one of five illegitimate sons of Sarah Lawrence (his father did not marry Sarah, as his wife refused to divorce him because they had four daughters). Lawrence was to become a charismatic legendary figure based on his desert exploits of the First World War in the Middle East. He was a very brave warrior, outstanding leader and highly intelligent. While many people adored him others, mainly those who had never met him, were critical of him. After the capture of Damascus during the First World War, Lawrence returned to England. He was awarded a Fellowship of All Souls College, Oxford, for the purpose of writing his famous book *Seven Pillars of Wisdom* (1926). He had completed most of the text, but while waiting at Reading Station to catch a train for Oxford he lost the bag containing the unpublished chapters of the original work. He decided to rewrite the text and moved to a room at Westminster, near the Houses of Parliament, that had been offered to him as a retreat by an architect.

Winston Churchill, who was at that time Secretary of State for the Colonies, invited Lawrence to become his assistant in the department responsible for the Middle East and be involved in the 1921 Cairo Conference convened to agree a settlement between the unsettled Arab factions who had not been pacified by the outcome of the Paris Peace Conference in 1919, which Lawrence had also attended.

After a period of negotiations in the Middle East where Lawrence was influential in creating the Kingdom of Jordan, Lawrence, now a kingmaker, returned to England and eventually resigned his government post; he then announced to his friends he wanted to join the Royal Air Force, not as an officer but as a ranker. Why he wanted to serve in the ranks is still open to question, although he had indicated to certain people that he no longer wanted any responsibility. It seems he also felt guilty that the Arabs had been betrayed by the allies regarding the desert revolt and their fight for freedom. His friends tried to dissuade him from enlisting, but with the help of influential people, including the Marshal of the Royal Air Force, Lawrence presented himself at the RAF recruiting office at Covent Garden, London, where with reluctance the staff accepted him as a recruit. After his basic training at the RAF Uxbridge depot he was sent to Farnborough on a photographic course. While there the national newspapers discovered he was in the RAF. The unwelcome publicity created by his presence resulted in the RAF deciding to discharge him from the service. Within two months of leaving the RAF he had joined the Army as a recruit in the Tank Corps at Bovington, Dorset, again by enlisting with the help of friends. During the time Lawrence was at Bovington he purchased Clouds Hill Cottage, Morton, located about a mile from the Army camp. This small cottage, now a National Trust property was to play an important part in his life.

Lawrence was unhappy in the Army and made repeated requests to be allowed back in the RAF. Such requests were refused, but eventually his wish was granted and he was again accepted into the RAF. Now a reborn aircraftman he was posted to RAF Cranwell in Lincolnshire. While at Cranwell he prepared *Revolt In The Desert*, published in 1927. This was not an original written text but was created by re-editing and using cut and paste skills to produce an abridged edition of *Seven Pillars of Wisdom*. So as to avoid unwanted publicity when the book was published Lawrence asked to be posted overseas. His new camp was at at Drigh Road, Karachi. While

Lawrence's introduction to Mount Batten, Plymouth, was when he disembarked from the SS Rajputana *on 2 February 1929. He used a rope ladder to climb down the side of the ship on to a small boat as a ploy to mislead the pressmen. He was taken to RAF Cattewater where he had breakfast, before travelling by train to London.*

The great natural harbour of Plymouth Sound. Here the SS Rajputana *anchored to allow Lawrence to disembark after his sea voyage from India.*

there Lawrence accepted a generous fee by an American publisher to translate Homer's *Odyssey*. The work on the translation was later to be associated with his activities while he was stationed at Mount Batten. He seemed relatively content in India, but was reposted again by his own request and sent to Peshawar, then on to what seemed like another planet, the remote station of Miranshah, near the Afghanistan border. While there his name was given as an arch spy who was involved in the political troubles of the region that were afoot. Lawrence's presence created a sensitive political situation. Although he was entirely innocent the RAF decided Lawrence must leave India; he was given a choice as to where he would like to be stationed and chose to return to Britain.

It had been hoped that his homecoming would not attract any attention, but when the liner arrived in Plymouth Sound the reporters from the national

newspapers were there in their hired boats waiting for him. He managed, with the assistance of Wing Commander Smith, to be taken to Mount Batten and from there he was driven to Newton Abbot Station where he caught a train to London. Lawrence stayed in the same small room at Westminster where in the early 1920s he had written most of his text for *Seven Pillars of Wisdom*. On his return to England he was presented with a new powerful Brough motorcycle paid for by Mrs Charlotte Shaw and others. This enabled him to visit his friends before he was given his new posting at RAF Cattewater, Plymouth.

Lawrence reported for duty at Mount Batten, one March afternoon in 1929. His billet was a First World War hut, one of many that stood close to the seashore, facing Plymouth Sound. There were 19 other airmen in his hut that had a coal-heated stove in the middle of the room. The scant furniture consisted of a table and forms, around the side were the airmen's folding beds, each with a locker above. Lawrence's bed was at the end of the hut by a window, through which he could see Plymouth Sound. The airman in charge of his hut was Corporal Tapper who had married into the Pascho family who lived at Turnchapel.

For many years after the First World War Lawrence continued to be a legendary hero. In the famous motion picture *Lawrence of Arabia*, a tall slim Peter O'Toole played the character of Lawrence. In reality, however, Lawrence was 5ft 5ins tall. Normally a quiet man he spoke with a soft Oxford accent and was as 'strong as an ox'.

The splendid interior of Deller's Café, Exeter, that Lawrence visited soon after arriving at Mount Batten. He mentioned this visit in a letter to an ex-colleague, Sydney Scanes.

George Bernard Shaw, Lord and Lady Astor and their daughter outside 3 Elliot Terrace, Plymouth Hoe, on their way to have lunch at RAF Mount Batten where they met up with Lawrence.

Lawrence and Work and Play

Stories circulated that when Lawrence was stationed at Plymouth he led the life of a recluse. Such tales are, however, completely unfounded. The myth was partly his doing as he wrote to his friends that he never went out of camp and they and the local newspapers believed him. During the first week of arriving at Mount Batten, he rode to Exeter on his Brough and visited the famous Deller's Café. A few weeks later when Lawrence was in Plymouth he was spotted by Lady Astor when she was out canvassing for a forthcoming election. Next day she contacted his commanding officer to get herself invited over to Mount Batten to meet Lawrence. Being a local Member of Parliament it would have been difficult for the Commanding Officer to refuse her request. Nancy, for that is what Lawrence called her, persuaded Lawrence there and then to go with her to Mount Gould to visit the newly built Astor Institute in Beaumont Road, which was one of her social interests. From here they motored on to the Virginian House Settlement, close to the Plymouth Barbican. The following day, the visit was published in a local newspaper. Lawrence was upset and wrote an irate letter to the Plymouth Guild of Social Services implying they were to blame for the publicity, but the incident passed.

Lady Astor (née Witcher Langhorne) was an American who, after her divorce from Robert Gould Shaw in 1903, had travelled to England with the hope of finding a suitable husband – a social venture not uncommon at the time. Here she met and married the American Waldorf Astor, one of the richest men in England at the time. Lord Astor was once a Member of Parliament for one of the constituencies of Plymouth. When he was raised to the peerage and could no longer serve as an MP, Nancy Astor was persuaded to be the Conservative candidate for the vacant seat. She won the by-election with votes from Plymouth's working-class and made history by becoming the first woman to take her seat in the House of Commons. She proved to be a vibrant and controversial MP who served Plymouth through peace and war.

Lady Astor would invite Lawrence to dinner at Elliot Terrace, the Astor's house on Plymouth Hoe. If he did not arrive on his Brough he would take a ferry and walk across Plymouth Hoe from Phoenix Wharf (at this period of time Madeira Road did not continue through to the Barbican, but rather pedestrians had to walk through a dark tunnel to get onto the Hoe). Elliot Terrace was a place where Lawrence could relax; he kept some of his books there and would call in even if Lady Astor was not in residence. If there was something physical about Lady Astor's relationship with Lawrence it was her pillion riding on his Brough motorcycle. He would take her riding around the Devon lanes and there is even a report of them speeding along the Embankment Road in Plymouth.

Soon after Lawrence had arrived at RAF Mount Batten he was given a weekend pass enabling him to accept an invitation from Lady Astor to St James's Square, London, to attend a reading by Bernard Shaw

Lawrences attic office where he worked and translated the Odyssey.

Station Stores where Lawrence kept his Brough and speed boat.

C/O Residence (Once the Castle Inn)

Flagstaff Quay (Now part remains)

Lawrence's Hut (Now public open space)

RAF Mount Batten C 1930

RAF Mount Batten in the early 1930s, indicating places associated with Lawrence when he was stationed there.

A letter from Wing Commander Sydney Smith referring to the assistance of Lawrence in the preparation of the Schneider Trophy event.

Charlie Chaplin in Plymouth, 1930, as a guest of Lady Astor. Lawrence was invited to dinner to meet him, but he refused the invitation. While in Plymouth, Chaplin attracted crowds of people when he visited the Barbican to watch 'The Blessing of the Fish'.

Lawrence on the slipway at RAF Calshot talking to British and Italian officers at the Schneider Trophy event in September 1929.

Lawrence standing on a float of the De Havilland Moth seaplane, he went flying in, c.1929. A Major Nathan owned and piloted the aircraft. They flew to many places in the South West including the Channel Islands.

of his new play *The Apple Cart*. There was another weekend break soon after, when Lawrence was invited by Basil Liddell Hart a well-known military writer of the period, to stay in Cornwall. Lawrence was collected from Mount Batten by car by Liddell Hart and his wife. After lunch at The Grand Hotel, Plymouth, they all set out for the Headland Hotel, Newquay. The hotel receptionist, looking at Lawrence who was wearing his airman's uniform of rough serge and a peak cap, was perhaps not familiar with his rankers' uniform, so asked Mrs Liddell Hart if her chauffeur would require a room. This 'chauffeur' was not only a legendary figure but arguably more steeped in military matters than any other General of the First World War!

Lawrence was attached to No. 204 Squadron and is is acknowledged on the request of his commanding officer to have designed the squadron's crest based on a cormorant displaying it wings while resting on a buoy in Plymouth Sound. First duties at Mount Batten were clerical, mainly typing station orders. Otherwise he assisted the boat crews, a kind of odd-job man, but this did not last for long. He complained in letters he wrote about the noise created by his hut mates, but in spite of this he seemed to get on well with them.

The news that Lawrence of Arabia was stationed at Mount Batten was of great excitement to the boys of

Hooe. On a Friday afternoon after school they would wait outside near St John's Church to see Lawrence, who was their hero, speed by on his motorcycle.

His commanding officer of RAF Mount Batten, Wing Commander Smith, was no stranger to Lawrence as they had previously met at the Cairo Conference and later at RAF Cranwell. During his first summer at Mount Batten Lawrence spent time flying in a converted Moth seaplane that belonged to Major Nathan, a friend of Sydney Smith. Nathan and Lawrence would fly along the coastline, sometimes landing in a bay. On one occasion they were compelled to land off Padstow, Cornwall, as the aircraft's petrol tank had sprung a leak.

Wing Commander Smith, who had been appointed to organise the prestigious 1929 Schneider Trophy event was aware of Lawrence's abilities and made him his assistant to help organise the event. Many people are not aware of the amount of planning for these races that was carried out at Mount Batten. Lawrence attended numerous meetings with Wing Commander Smith that were held in London, Calshot and Portsmouth. If a meeting was held in London, the two men would catch the night train from Plymouth. Wing Commander Smith would travel in a first-class sleeping compartment and stay in a hotel, whereas Lawrence the ranker travelled in a third-class carriage. He would take a cushion on which to rest his head and used the ploy of pulling the compartment's blinds down to deter anyone else from entering. Arriving at Paddington Station Lawrence travelled across London and stayed at the Union Jack Club near Waterloo Station, while Wing Commander Smith made for the RAF Club.

Above: *The RAF Mount Batten workshops showing the door where Lawrence kept his Brough motorcycle and his speedboat. Above the door is the attic he used as an office and where he spent considerable time translating the* Odyssey.

Left: *Amy Johnson, the pioneer aviator, in the cockpit of a Moth aircraft. Johnson landed a Moth aircraft on the United Services Golf Club next to the Mount Batten seaplane station.*

RECORD OF FLIGHTS.

Date.	Aircraft.		Pilot.	Journey.	Time in Air.		Remarks.
	Type.	Markings.			Hrs.	Mins.	
				Solo.			
				Brought forward...	58	40	
Dec. 13	Moth	BN	Self.	Stag Lane.	00	25	General
"	"	"	"	"	00	15	" C.S. Humphries passenger.
" 14	"	"	"	"	00	50	"
"	"	"	"	"	00	50	"
" 15	"	"	"	"	00	45	"
" 17	"	LJ.	"	Stag Lane to Plymouth	02	10	Major Hallam passenger
1930 Jan. 8	"	YV	"	" - Brooklands	01	30	Major Hallam's machine
" 9	"	"	"	" " " Hamble	02	15	(with passenger)
				Carried forward...	67	40	

Amy Johnson's flight log recording her flight from Stag Lane, Middlesex, to Mount Batten, on 17 December 1929.

Flete House, South Hams, where Lawrence dined with Lord Mildmay and other peers of the realm. Here at Flete, Lawrence met Russell Page who was later to become a famous international garden designer. Lawrence helped Page design the water garden at Flete which still exists.

One Sunday morning in July 1929 Lawrence rode across Dartmoor on his Brough motorcycle to visit Henry Williamson at his home in North Devon; they had never met before. Williamson, arguably the leading nature writer at the time, had been intrigued with the text of *Seven Pillars Wisdom*, while Lawrence when he was out in India, had written a critique of *Tarka the Otter*, a book that impressed him. This was the beginning of a friendship between the two men that later was to end in a dramatic way linked to Lawrence's death.

Nearer the time of the start of the Schneider Trophy races, Lawrence and his commanding officer moved to Calshot. The RAF Headquarters was on a steam yacht that had been offered as a facility by the banker Colin Cooper. While at Calshot, Lawrence came close to being discharged from the RAF again; he had been seen talking to high-ranking officers, including Marshall Balbo who was in charge of the Italian racing team. The consequence of this was that Lawrence was reprimanded and a list of names was drawn up of famous people that he was forbid-

den to be in contact with – that included Lady Astor.

At Mount Batten, Lawrence continued his translation of Homer's *Odyssey*, a task that would earn him money to use towards the repair work on his Dorset cottage. Wing Commander Smith had allocated Lawrence an attic room above the station's workshop reached by a steep wooden staircase; this acted as his office and gave him privacy. On 1 October 1929 the name RAF Cattewater was changed to RAF Mount Batten, brought about by the suggestion of Wing Commander Smith and Lawrence, putting aside Lawrence's preference of retaining the historic Danish flavour of the original name.

During the Schneider Trophy event, the steam yacht *Karen* was used as the official RAF headquarters. The yacht carried a speedboat that Cooper had purchased from Sir Henry Segrave, when the famous driver was in America. Cooper allowed Lawrence to use the boat to carry people from the yacht to Calshot. The speedboat was a very powerful craft and Cooper's wife emplored her husband to give the speedboat away before he had an accident with it.

Cooper, seeing how well Lawrence handled the boat, offered it to him as a present, that was accepted. The speedboat was duly delivered to Lawrence at Mount Batten a few days later. The *Karen* sailed into Plymouth Sound with the speedboat suspended from a cradle and the craft was lowered into the water. Jimmy Lillicrap, who lived on the Plymouth Barbican and who was related to the Turnchapel Lillicraps, had been retained by Lawrence as his ferryman. Jimmy rowed Lawrence out to the speedboat, and Lawrence then steered it back to Mount Batten.

At the end of 1929, Major Nathan sold his Moth seaplane. He purchased another Moth aircraft and asked Wing Commander Sydney Smith if he could fly it to Mount Batten to have an extended fuel tank fitted to it. (The moth aircraft could be converted back to a land plane by replacing the floats with wheels). Lawrence was given the task of assisting the Moth to land. He used a smoke bomb to indicate to the pilot the direction of the wind and the aircraft landed on the course of the United Services Golf Club that in 1929 was situated adjacent to the flying boat station. As Lawrence went up to greet Nathan a woman climbed out of the pilot's seat. To his amazement it was the pioneer English aviator Amy Johnson. Major Nathan had got to know Johnson at Stag Lane, Middlesex, the home of the De Havilland flying club; she used to go there to have flying lessons. Nathan, realising her wish to obtain experience in cross-country flying, offered her the opportunity to fly his Moth from Stag Lane to Mount Batten. This was the longest journey thus far that she had piloted. In 1930 Johnson became the first woman to fly solo from London to Australia.

Lawrence would travel over to Plymouth to visit the city's central Post Office or drive over to Devonport to buy his special writing paper and type-writer ribbons. Early in 1930 he began to socialise outside the camp. He accepted Lord Mildmay's invitation to go with Wing Commander Smith and his wife to dine at Flete House. The guest list included peers of the realm. After dinner everyone retired to the drawing-room to listen to Clare Smith sing, in German, the songs of Schubert and Brahms (she had been coached by Lawrence who spoke the language).

Lawrence visited Flete House on other occasions as he had made friends with Russell Page, a young gardener who had been commissioned by Lord Mildmay to design the gardens at Flete. Lawrence helped Page plan the water garden that still exists at Flete House. He and Page, with members of the

Lawrence collecting his Brough Superior after it had been serviced at Nottingham, c.1930. He is talking to George Brough who had built Lawrence's powerful machine. This was the model Lawrence rode when he was stationed at RAF Mount Batten.

Mildmay family, would go for walks in the extensive grounds of Flete. Russell Page went on to become a famous international designer and one of his displays was used for the layout of the postwar Festival of Britain gardens at Battersea Park.

The Nature of a Legend

Exactly what menial tasks Lawrence carried out at Mount Batten as an aircraftman is difficult to ascertain. He was known to be a duty orderly that meant changing the bed sheets on a Wednesday for the men in his hut. He was also required to collect coal in a bucket to heat the hut's stove. One airman who was in the same hut as Lawrence remembered that Lawrence was 'always where he wanted to be'. There is no evidence that Lawrence was antisocial, at least not when he was stationed at Mount Batten. He would go to the NAAFI canteen on a Thursday evening and treat his hut colleagues to tea and buns. When on fire picquet duty Lawrence would jump on his motorcycle to go and buy fish and chips for his colleagues.

Lawrence got to know Turnchapel well; he would call in to the small grocery shop at the top of the hill to pay his bills for goods he had bought. It was also the shop to which the airmen brought their laundry. Lawrence employed Mrs Carpenter, a local Turnchapel women to do his weekly washing. Once a week she would make her way to Mount Batten,

Spooner's Corner, Plymouth. During the 1930s Lawrence would come to this area. On one occasion he did some shopping for Clare Smith at Boots the Chemist, the shop next to Lawry's.

A group of friends and family taken by the flagstaff, Mount Batten, c.1930. Lawrence is pictured with Clare Smith to his left. The young girl is Clare Smith's daughter.

pushing a pram with her baby in it, to collect Lawrence's washing and deliver his clean shirts and underwear. Another Turnchapel resident, Mrs Tucker, who owned the grocery store in the village would each morning take a small barrow containing newspapers and deliver them to the flying boat station. On one occasion the weather was so bad the wind blew some of the copies into the water. Lawrence happened to be nearby and retrieved the newspapers that were soaked. To compensate for the loss, Lawrence counted out the number of newspapers that had been ruined and paid Mrs Tucker the value of them out of his own pocket. This was the nature of the man.

Lawrence was still stationed in India when he was first contacted by Francis Yeats-Brown, deputy editor of *The Spectator,* to ask him if he would be interested in some freelance work. Soon after Lawrence returned to England he met Yeats Brown in London. During the Whitsun holiday of 1930, Yeats-Brown travelled to Devon and stayed at a hotel at Yelverton and from here drove to Mount Batten to visit Lawrence. On the Whit Sunday the two men drove out to Dartmoor. Yeats-Brown had received the printer's proofs of his book *Bengal Lancer* and asked Lawrence if he would read them. Lawrence, laying on the moors, started to correct the text. Yeats-Brown watched Lawrence rapidly flick over the pages; he had never seen anyone read so quickly. Yeats-Brown decided to go for a walk and when he returned Lawrence handed the proof pages back to him. They had been corrected and marked up in the style

adopted by a professional proof reader. Later the rights were sold to Hollywood who made the film *The Lives of a Bengal Lancer,* which was a box-office success in 1935.

Lawrence would visit Plymouth with his commanding officer, taking the Smiths' dogs with them. Lawrence would stop in the streets and talk to people he knew. There was nothing of the recluse about him. Mrs Hanika, who with her husband managed Genois, a popular Swiss restaurant in the city recalls that Lawrence, dressed in his RAF uniform, would arrive at Genois for an evening meal, sometime eating alone, other times with a friend; he had his own corner table reserved for him. It was a similar situation in the dining hall at RAF Mount Batten; because of his reputation Lawrence had his own unofficial reserved table and chair, that no other airmen would use. He would often sit there on his own surrounded by the daily newspapers. Some evenings he would go to Wing Commander Smith's residence, the 'Fishermans Arms' as Lawrence would call it, and have a cooked meal with the Smiths. Lawrence and Clare Smith would listen to classical music on the electric gramophone he brought to the house. They spent hours together in the drawing-room entranced by the music, while Sydney Smith would go over to the officers' mess.

Lawrence worked on his speedboat that he kept in the station stores. He and Clare Smith had named the boat *Biscuit.* Satisfied it was in good running order, he began to take the *Biscuit* out across water. He would travel across Plymouth Sound to visit Lord

Lawrence was a friend of Lord and Lady Edgcumbe. He would travel across Plymouth Sound in his speedboat with Clare Smith to Mount Edgcumbe and walk in the estate gardens.

Left: *Lawrence speeding in the* Biscuit *out in Plymouth Sound, c.1930, with Corporal Tapper who was married to a Turnchapel girl.*

Lawrence in his working overalls on Flagstaff Quay, c.1930.

The cottage of the Ash family at Brunel Terrace, Saltash, where Lawrence was taken after being rescued by Arthur Ash and where he slept in the downstairs front room.

Above: *The model of Drake's Golden Hind constructed by Lawrence and Wing Commander Smith when they were stationed at Mount Batten.*

Right: *Lawrence in his white robes at a desert camp in the Middle East. He has his critics but they all agree he was a very brave person. During the First World War he was recommended for the Victoria Cross. This characteristic of the man was shown during his gallant rescue attempt at the 1931 flying boat disaster in Plymouth Sound.*

Clare Smith and Lawrence pose on the quay which is still opposite the Mount Batten Centre, c.1930.

Lawrence and Clare Smith's favourite river trip was to make for the Tamar, then navigate the River Lynher and take the Biscuit under the railway bridge seen in the picture to Poldrissick, to picnic in a disused quarry. This area of east Cornwall is still an area of unspoilt beautiful countryside and tranquillity.

Left: *Clare Smith and friends prepared for a picnic and Lawrence holding the painter of the Biscuit, about to depart on one of their river trips.*

Below: *A snapshot taken of Clare Smith, Lawrence and the Hon. Montague Vere Eliot at St Germans Quay, c.1931.*

When visiting the Earl of St Germans at Port Eliot, Lawrence and Clare Smith would tie the Biscuit up at St Germans Quay. Then Lawrence called at the quaymaster's cottage for a 'wash and brush up' before walking through the estate grounds to meet the earl. This picture of the cottage was taken in 2004.

Children at play in the Barbican area of Plymouth. E.M. Forster, author of A Passage to India, *visited Lawrence at Mount Batten. They spent their time walking around, looking at the old buildings on the Barbican, or visiting the gardens at Mount Edgcumbe.*

and Lady Edgcumbe at Mount Edgcumbe House or make for Cothele House.

One night Harry Ash, a salmon fisherman who worked the Tamar had laid his nets and was waiting at Caver Beach when he heard what he thought was an aeroplane engine suddenly stop. He peered through the darkness and saw that a boat was stuck on a mud bank. He rowed out to find a man who was dressed in RAF uniform: Lawrence introduced himself. The fisherman took him and his boat back to Saltash. Being late at night Ash invited Lawrence into his cottage, where he slept in the front room. The outcome of this nocturnal meeting was that Lawrence was invited to go salmon fishing. He would arrive at Saltash on his Brough and park it outside the terraced cottage. The neighbours never knew this was the same man who 13 years earlier had led a small band of tribesmen across 600 miles of desert in the most remote conditions, returning alone on his tracks in the scorching desert heat to rescue a lost Arab and then travelling on to capture, what was deemed impossible, the Red Sea port of Aqaba from the Turks. This feat was to alter the outcome of the

war in the Middle East. Lawrence seemed to like fishing and Clare Smith recorded how she and Lawrence would spend time at Mount Batten Breakwater fishing for mackerel, she baiting the spinner for him.

Lawrence and Clare Smith had been invited by Lady Edgcumbe to Cothele house that was used for social occasions. Lawrence suggested to Clare Smith they should make the journey up the River Tamar in his speedboat; they tied up the *Biscuit* alongside Cothele Quay. As Lady Edgcumbe showed her guests around the rooms of Cothele, in one bedroom Lawrence noticed a small rug under a hip bath. He examined it and turned to his hostess and told her in his opinion this was a rare and valuable hunting rug and if he was correct, there were only three others in existence. Lawrence suggested to Lady Edgcumbe that she should get the rug valued and this she did; she received confirmation that the rug was as rare as Lawrence suspected.

During the summer of 1930 Lawrence visited Dartington Hall, Totnes, to meet Leonard Elmhirst who, with his wife, had a few years earlier opened a progressive school at Dartington that attracted considerable publicity and criticism. In complete contrast to this excursion, Lawrence attended the annual Wembury Regatta in 1930 and raced his boat against a small hydroplane called 'Nippy 111', that belonged to Mr Skentelbery, a Stonehouse boat-builder. Lawrence returned from Wembury by road to Mount Batten. The other airmen who had partici-pated in the regatta set off in their boats to return to camp but owing to the poor weather became stranded by the Mew Stone, the giant mass of rock that protrudes from the sea near the mouth of the River Yealm. This is the rock that Charles Kingsley refers to in his 1863 publication *The Water Babies* as the place where the 'Mayor of Plymouth came 800–900 years ago to look for lobsters'. Eventually Plymouth's lifeboat was called out to guide the airmen back to Mount Batten.

Lawrence and Clare Smith had established a close relationship. When Lawrence worked on his transla-tion of Homer's *Odyssey* up in his attic office, Clare Smith would bring a flask of coffee and sit in silence with him during the evening while he worked. Clare's marriage to Wing Commander Smith was unhappy, in part due to her devotion to Lawrence. She records in a letter deposited at the British Library that they saw each other every day when Lawrence was at the camp. He would take her in the *Biscuit*

Lawrence with his Commanding Officer, Wing Commander Sydney Smith, photographed on holiday at Thurlestone in 1930.

The Sydney Smiths invited Lawrence to have a holiday with them at Thurlestone in 1930. This picture taken in the porch of the house they stayed in, shows Lawrence with three women. On the right is Clare Smith. The house stands close to the seashore, where Lawrence and Clare would go shrimping in the rock pools.

Lawrence on the deck of HMS Norfolk, the occasion being the commissioning of the cruiser at Devonport in May 1930.

Lawrence with Scott-Paine, the powerboat builder, whose yard was at Hythe. Lawrence was seconded to Hythe from Mount Batten to be involved in the development of the powerboat RAF 200.

Corporal Leonard Mitcham, stationed at RAF Mount Batten, would go fishing with Lawrence and Claude Mears who lived above a boathouse at Turnchapel. Mitcham achieved the rank of Wing Commander, and he requested that, when he died, his ashes should be scattered on the water from Mount Batten.

In 1930, while stationed at Mount Batten, Lawrence visited Radford House, Hooe, where Sir Walter Raleigh was detained before he was sent to London to be executed. Raleigh was a kinsman of Lawrence. During his visit, Lawrence came across an ancient relic he believed was a Roman altar.

Lawrence at the wheel of RAF 200 in Plymouth Sound, 1931. This is the prototype boat Lawrence is associated with in the development of the craft for air-sea rescue.

across Plymouth Sound to Mount Edgcumbe and there they would wander through the extensive grounds admiring the beautiful flowering shrubs. According to Clare Smith there were many river picnics. She had embroidered two cushions with their initials that they used when they when out in the boat. Off they would go, from Flagstaff Quay at Mount Batten towards the River Tamar making for the Lynher River. Along the upper stretches of the river is Poldrissick where they discovered an old quarry where they would sit and relax. On one of their river trips along the Lynher they came across a small dilapidated bungalow at Drillers Quay. On return visits, when it was raining, they would sit under the verandah and have their picnic. There was an occasion when they missed the tide whilst returning to Mount Batten. The *Biscuit* became stuck on a mud bank, so for most of the night the pair had no option but to sit in the boat and wait for the tide to rise. Another place in East Cornwall they visited was Port Eliot the home of the Earl of St Germans. Lawrence would bring the *Biscuit* up to St Germans Quay, where the quaymaster would be waiting, having heard the noise of the approaching engine. After tying up the boat, Lawrence would go into the

quaymaster's cottage and have 'a wash and brush up' in the back kitchen. Then he and Clare would take a long walk in the grounds of the estate to visit the Earl. There were times when Lawrence visited Port Eliot on his own to meet up with friends, such as George Bernard Shaw and Sir Ronald Storrs, the latter associated with Lawrence in the Middle East during the First World War and mentioned in *Seven Pillars of Wisdom*.

Lawrence's visitors at RAF Mount Batten included E.M. Forster, famous for novels that included *A Passage to India*. Forster knew Plymouth, he had a great-aunt who lived in Manamead, north of the city. Forster observed that Lawrence tended to socialise with the officers rather than the rankers. The two men walked the streets of Plymouth, particularly in the Barbican area examining the many old buildings. They also visited Mount Edgcumbe and spent time walking through the gardens admiring the shrubs and the panoramic views.

Throughout most of 1930 Lawrence paid more attention in his free time to his speedboat than he did to his translation of Homer, which set back the publication date. During the summer months of 1930 Lawrence seemed to be contented with his life, although he

It is known that Lawrence lodged at No. 2 Oak Cottage, Plymstock, in the latter part of his posting to RAF Mount Batten. Each day he would take his motorcycle and drive down to the flying boat station.

rarely admitted he was a happy person. His socialising continued in and around Plymouth. He went with the Sydney Smiths to the commissioning of the cruiser HMS *Norfolk* at Devonport. There were many other invitations he accepted, including dining at The Terrace, Devonport, Admiralty House and Government House, where he met the local society and senior military officers from all the services.

Scott Paine, a well-known powerboat builder, convinced the Air Ministry he could design more powerful and cheaper boats than those used by the RAF. A distinctive feature of his design was that the boat would be built on the principle of a planing hull (designed to float on water), in contrast to the more traditional displacement hull. A prototype was built at The British Powerboat Company, Hythe, Hampshire. The craft designated RAF 200 underwent preliminary trials. Soon after the inquest of the flying boat disaster Lawrence travelled to Hythe to be inducted into the workings of RAF 200. Further extensive trials were needed, which were carried out from Mount Batten. Lawrence was chosen as one of the crew members. The testing procedure included

taking the boat out into the English Channel and travelling down the coast to the Scilly Isles. Lawrence was now more a mariner than an airman.

Times were changing. Wing Commander Smith had been promoted to Group Captain and was to take over Command at RAF Manston, Kent. His wife, who seemed reluctant to go, eventually joined him. Lawrence took two weeks' leave to travel with Clare to her new home in Kent and to help her and Sydney Smith settle into their new home. It seems that because of Clare Smith's demands on him, Lawrence started to distance himself from her. That said there were still occasions when they met up at Salcombe, where Clare Smith stayed with friends in a grand house on the North Sands side of the town. On such occasions they took the opportunity to go back to Mount Batten and take the *Biscuit* out to visit their favourite haunts up the River Lynher.

After a period of working away from Plymouth, Lawrence was ordered to report back to Mount Batten where he was put on routine tasks. This seemed to make him rather unhappy as he wanted more job satisfaction, so he applied for his discharge from the RAF. He had been preparing to leave, having taken many of his belongings from Mount Batten to Clouds Hill, when the Air Ministry offered him work to oversee the building and testing of RAF marine craft. Such a role involved being transferred from RAF Mount Batten. The sensitive nature of his presence meant in his new role he was to go about his work in civilian clothes. He left RAF Mount Batten to report at RAF Felixstowe, from there he was billeted at the Isle of Wight, Portsmouth and Southampton. Later he was transferred to Bridlington where he stayed for a short period of time, overseeing the maintenance of boats before his discharge from the RAF.

Lawrence returned to live at his cottage at Clouds Hill. On 13 May 1935, two months into his retirement, he was involved in his fatal motorcycle accident and died at Bovington Camp Hospital on 19 May. Clare Smith was in Singapore and did not attend his funeral. He was buried at Moreton, Dorset.

An aerial view of RAF Mount Batten showing the camouflaged round tower. The warship at anchor is HMS Newcastle, a familiar sight to Plymouthians during the Plymouth Blitz, as it was used to supplement the anti-aircraft defences.

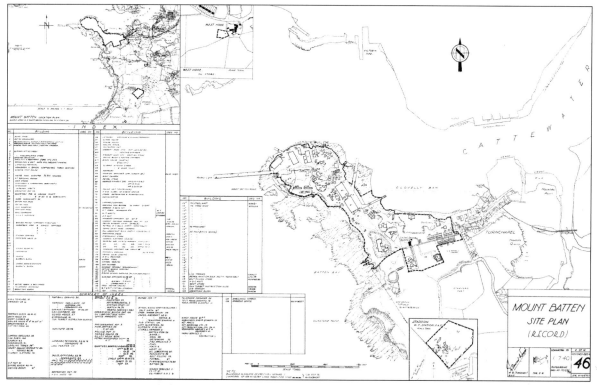

A plan of RAF Mount Batten during the first year of the Second World War. Gone are most of the original wooden huts that have been replaced with brick buildings.

Chapter 5

RAF Mount Batten in the Second World War

Sunderlands Make Their Mark

In the months prior to the Second World War No. 204 Squadron of the Royal Airforce based at Mount Batten had been supplied with the new Short Sunderland flying boats. In design, size and performance the aircraft was completely different from other RAF flying boats. The name Short can be misleading, for the aircraft was a huge monoplane powered by four engines; the plane was named for the Short brothers who were instrumental in its design and development. The Sunderland, so elegant in flight, was a pleasure to watch. There are those who say the Sunderland flying boat had a form equal to that of the legendary Spitfire.

The Sunderland flew with a crew of 13 men. In terms of accommodation the plane itself was self-sufficient with a wardroom (a space for the use of commissioned officers), bunks, a galley where bacon, chops and potatoes could be cooked. There was also a wash-basin and toilet. In charge was the captain and the first pilot was the man who would bring the aircraft back if the captain was injured or dead. There was also another pilot on board. The navigator, the essential brain behind any operation, would be positioned in the plastic navigation 'bubble' up on top of the aircraft. The wireless operator mechanic, was a signals man and had the technical skills to make repairs. The flight engineer would monitor the performance of the engines and the fuel, assisted by a fitter. A Sunderland would also carry up to three wireless operators, who also served as gunners. In charge was a senior gunner, any known crack shot serving with the Australians would sit in the rear gun turret.

Each crew member of a Sunderland flying boat was required to be both a competent aviator and a seaman. On the water they would need to be able to control the flying boat in currents and fast-moving tides as well as counter the forces of wind that blew

A Sunderland flying boat on the concourse outside one of the hangars. Across the Cattewater is Cattedown.

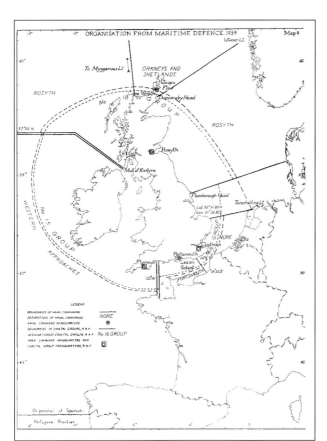

The maritime defence of the United Kingdom at the outbreak of war. At this time the headquarters of No. 15 Group RAF Coastal Command was based at Mount Batten.

The RAAF pilot's room at Mount Batten in March 1940.

against the hull. If the crew lost control the Sunderland could be driven ashore – at Mount Batten this could mean being dashed upon rocks.

The early deliveries of Sunderlands at Mount Batten were camouflaged in green and brown with black paint underneath the wings. Later this colour scheme was changed to silver and then sky blue.

On Sunday 3 September 1939, the day war was declared, the operational strength at RAF Mount Batten stood at six Sunderland aircraft. There were no other operational air bases in South West England other than RAF Mount Batten. Reports had already been received at the station that enemy submarines had been seen, resulting in an active patrol duty being introduced. No. 204 Squadron was soon out in the Western Approaches escorting homecoming ships. From the very beginning of hostilities German U-boats had started attacking allied shipping. Nine days into the war a Mount Batten Sunderland pilot reported that the SS *Kensington Court*, which had been carrying a cargo of grain, had been sunk 70 miles from the Isles of Scilly by gunfire from U-35. Eventually two Sunderlands from Pembroke Dock arrived on the scene. Flight Lieutenant Barrett of No.

204 Squadron and another Sunderland, despite the dangerous conditions, descended and landed alongside a lifeboat. This was the first air-sea rescue of the war and 34 survivors were saved. The rescued crew members of SS *Kensington Court* landed at Mount Batten and for his gallant action in this operation Barrett was awarded the Distinguished Flying Cross.

On 17 September 1939 the aircraft carrier HMS *Courageous*, which only a few days before had sailed from Plymouth, was torpedoed by U-29 and sank within 15 minutes. Over 500 of her crew, including many Devon men, were lost. This is the period (September 1939–April 1940) of the conflict that some historians describe as the phoney war, as there was comparatively little action.

RAF Mount Batten suffered early casualties when, in October 1939 a patrolling Sunderland flying boat of No. 204 Squadron crashed outside Plymouth Sound due to bad visibility. Four members of the crew were killed and seven others were seriously injured. One of the crew, Flying Officer D. Fork, is buried in the churchyard at Hooe.

At the start of the war No. 204 Squadron began patrols over the English Channel and Western Approaches. In April 1940 the squadron was moved to the Shetlands in order to carry out patrols off Norway. Then in April 1941 No. 204 Squadron was transferred to Iceland.

No. 10 Squadron (RAAF) Arrives

No. 204 Squadron was replaced with No. 10 Squadron of the Royal Australian Airforce (RAAF) that, except for a seven-month detachment to Pembroke Dock, South Wales, during 1941, served at Mount Batten for the duration of the war. Members of the RAAF had

Above: *A Short Sunderland flying boat from RAF Mount Batten showing its graceful form flying across the Mew Stone, near Wembury, South Devon.*

Below: *The sinking of the* Lancastria *off St Nazaire, 1940. A total of 6,000 servicemen are reported to have lost their lives. The survivors were landed at Falmouth and Millbay docks. All surviving RAF personnel were taken to RAF Mount Batten.*

The funeral of Flight Sergeant Oliver of No. 10 Squadron RAAF who was buried on 2 May 1940 at the Parish Church of St John the Evangelist, Hooe. Revd E. Bridger leads the bearer party comprising three RAAF and three RAF Flight Sergeants.

Right: *The gravestone of Flight Sergeant Oliver at St John's churchyard, Hooe.*

This rare picture records the Mount Batten Breakwater broken in two after being hit by an enemy bomb. When it came to be repaired it was discovered that there was an internal wooden framework.

Part of the air defences of Plymouth were the barrage balloons that were flown to reduce the airspace and prevent low-level air attack. No. 934 Balloon Squadron was based at Mount Batten. One of these giant inflatables was sited at Mount Batten's Breakwater.

The RAF Mount Batten Breakwater, with anti-submarine bombs being loaded onto a lighter to be transferred to a Sunderland flying boat, 1940.

originally arrived in England before the war in order to be trained in the use of flying Sunderland aircraft. The flying boats had been ordered by the RAAF, so these men were to learn how to fly them, then fly them home. However, production problems delayed the delivery of their flying boats and while the Australian pilots waited for their aircraft to be delivered they trained at Pembroke Dock. In October 1939 when the airmen were ready to fly back to Australia, the squadron received an order to remain in England with a notification that other members of the RAAF were on their way to join them. These Australians arrived to face the severest winter England had experienced for 75 years. Throughout the bitterly cold weather of 1939 the Australians built up their flying boat squadron. In April 1940 they moved to Mount Batten and became operational.

Australians who were posted to RAAF No. 10 Squadron were regarded as something special. Flying a Sunderland was a special honour that came to very few. The pilots were young men; some had left school and gone straight into the Air Force. However, traditional attitudes were at this time entrenched in the service. Noncommissioned aircrew only saw officer crew when they arrived on board and during departure from the aircraft; there was little or no social interaction.

In the second week of May 1940 the German Army invaded Holland. Soon after their Blitzkrieg tactics swept through Northwest Europe, which ended with the capitulation of France. During the 1940 evacuation of the British Expeditionary Force from Dunkirk the Mount Batten Sunderlands carried out escort duties. French servicemen arrived in Plymouth with some of them passing through RAF Mount Batten. Following the defeat of the allies on the continent and the expected forthcoming invasion of England all No. 10 Squadron personnel were recalled from leave, and operational sorties were increased. At Mount Batten defensive measures were introduced. For example ground personnel were trained in the use of rifles or machine-guns. As the Germans occupied the French airfields and Channel ports, German submarines could now, as in the First World War, operate close to Britain without having to return to the shipyards of Germany. The German U-boats lost no time in making for the southwestern region of the English Channel, where they lay in wait off the Devon coast, close to the approaches of Plymouth, to attack any allied shipping. As the German Army advanced through Northern France allied troops made for the port of St Nazaire to be evacuated back to England.

A Disaster Unfolds

Mount Batten was linked to the catastrophic events that were about to take place. On 15 June 1940, a former Cunard liner, the *Lancastria*, anchored in Plymouth Sound. For the people who came to the Hoe, this was just another ship that added to the familiar maritime scene. The *Lancastria* was, however, at Plymouth on a special mission: waiting for orders to sail to St Nazaire in Brittany, in order to bring home troops and refugees, as part of the allied withdrawal from France. The liner sailed out of the Sound, and within two days of her departure was to be involved in one of Britain's worst maritime disasters. When just 5 miles off the coast of St Nazaire, loaded with some 6,000 servicemen and civilians, the *Lancastria* was attacked by German aircraft. It is thought this action resulted in the loss of around 3,000 lives, although the exact number has never been known. The survivors were taken in rescue ships to Falmouth, Cornwall and Millbay Dock, Plymouth. It is believed over 1,000 airmen were on board the *Lancastria* when she was hit; those who survived were later brought to RAF Mount Batten.

Only a couple of days after the sinking of the *Lancastria* an RAAF Sunderland from Mount Batten sighted and attacked a U-boat. Two weeks after that another Australian Sunderland sank U-26.

Secret Missions

RAF Mount Batten's operation book records that on 21 June 1940, Walrus L2312 of No. 10 Squadron RAAF on special duty was overdue and posted as missing. This was the first casualty of the RAAF Squadron.

On 18 June 1940 the Supermarine Walrus had flown from Mount Batten on a daring secret involving British Intelligence, Winston Churchill and General de Gaulle. Its destination was Brittany and its mission was to deliver a British secret agent and save the wife and family of General de Gaulle, the Free French leader domiciled in England, from the advancing German motorised troops. Exactly what happened to the plane is not known. The weather was bad and the aircraft could have been lost in the fog that covered the countryside. There is also a suggestion that it was intercepted by an enemy fighter. A Madame Pengam recalls seeing an aircraft on fire in the vicinity, and whatever the cause, the Walrus certainly crashed, killing the crew. Wreckage and bodies were later found at Keranou in France. After the disappearance of the Walrus another attempt was made by the Special Operations Executive, this time using a motor torpedo boat to collect Madame de Gaulle and her children, only to find that they had caught the last boat to leave Brest and had arrived safely in England.

Another secret mission started from Mount Batten on 18 June, when a Sunderland carrying VIP passengers, including the Secretary of State for the Colonies, Lord Lloyd, a personal friend of the late Lawrence of Arabia. His quest was to try to persuade the French Government to continue the fight against the Germans. The destination was Lake Biscarosse from where Lord Lloyd would travel to Bordeaux. His visit was in vain as the French decided to capitulate.

Mount Batten became the sole link between England and the Middle East resulting in No. 1 Air Dispatch and Receipt Unit being established there. From here VIPs were flown to Gibraltar and North Africa. During the war many famous and important people passed through RAF Mount Batten.

Under Attack

In the summer of 1940, at the time of the Battle of Britain, Plymouth was within flying distance of the German Airforce. During the first week of July, Plymouth experienced its first air raid, within two weeks the city was bombed on numerous occasions. In mid-July other than the air raids on Plymouth, the German Airforce attacked RAF Mount Batten, causing significant damage, including the destruction of the airmen's mess. As part of the enemy's invasion plans, Plymouth was one of the ports on the South Coast that it was attempting to seal off. To this end, the Germans lay magnetic mines in the waters of Plymouth Sound and the Hamoaze.

Plymouth, as part of its air defences flew, barrage balloons. In June 1941 a barrage balloon unit was formed at Mount Batten and operated nine moorings. When not closely hauled they flew high in the sky around Plymouth. Some balloons, as the German pilots noted, were linked to each other. These silver inflated monsters were intended to deny the enemy air space and prevent or deter enemy aircraft from attacking their targets. The cable that held the balloon was capable of ripping off the wing of an aircraft, as some did. Unfortunately the barrage balloon did not distinguished friend from foe, which meant that the airspace around Plymouth was never entirely the RAAF's own – it was perilous up there for friend and foe alike. This was demonstrated when, later in the war, Sunderland ML848 hit a barrage balloon cable when flying over Plymouth Sound. Fortunately it managed to alight safely.

The magnetic mines dropped in Plymouth Sound caused the Royal Navy and the Royal Australian Air Force considerable problems regarding how best to deal with them. The German minelaying operations at Plymouth led to routine minesweeping operations in the waters of the Sound, which had to be carried out each time any flying boats took off on an operational mission.

There was a reduction in the daylight raids during September as the Germans were planning to destroy the United Kingdom's industrial economic capacity, as well as terrorise and demoralise the British people. The threat of an invasion of England had diminished, but had not been dismissed. On 7 and 8 September 1940 Mount Batten recorded two invasion alerts. It was during September that a Sunderland on patrol sighted survivors from the *City of Benares*. This passenger ship, which had been taking evacuee adults and children from Britain to Canada, had been torpedoed in the Atlantic. Only 13 of the 90 children on board survived the attack.

On 27 and 28 November 1940 the German Airforce attacked RAF Mount Batten destroying one of the large flying boat hangars and two Sunderland aircraft. Nearby the large round tanks that stood by Hooe Lake and close to the Turnchapel railway

RAF Mount Batten was attacked by the German Air Force on 28 November 1940, destroying two Sunderland flying boats and one of the large hangars. The black plume of smoke is from the Turnchapel oil tanks that had been set on fire by enemy aircraft.

station, stored and supplied oil for the Royal Navy. During the Mount Batten raid of 27 November an enemy aircraft dropped a bomb on one of the tanks at Turnchapel that set the oil on fire. The burning oil created a huge plume of dense smoke that hung like a great pall above Plymouth, visible for miles around. It was feared this would attract more enemy aircraft to come and bomb the area. The intense heat that was generated caused the water being directed on to the fire to evaporate. Three firemen lost their lives fighting the blaze, while others saved themselves by jumping into the water. The blazing oil destroyed the small Turnchapel railway station and spilt over into Hooe Lake. Families were evacuated from Hooe to Plymstock and later the village was evacuated to Plympton.

At Radford, not far from the Turnchapel Naval oil depot, there were Air Ministry fuel tanks. These were built in 1938 and came into use in 1940. Pipelines had been laid from Turnchapel jetty that extended up Murder Hill and then down to Radford.

An underground pump was used to deliver the fuel to the tanks. These tanks survived the war without being hit by bombs. Later on in the war Thankes Naval oil tanks at Torpoint, Cornwall, were attacked and set on fire. The loss of the oil from these depots meant that the Navy had lost most of its oil reserves in South West England.

A Valiant Contribution

The operations of Coastal Command can be thought of as a continuation of operations that were started by the RNAS during the First World War, although by the time of the Second World War, it was all on a much bigger scale. The attack on allied shipping was an indication of how serious a threat the German submarines could be to the country's lifeblood and measures had to be taken to counter this threat. The use of flying boats from Mount Batten for combating the submarine menace was vital, but it should be emphasised that Mount Batten's involvement in the nation's defence was only a part of the huge anti-submarine operation. The Coastal Command bases in Cornwall, Devon and South Wales were an important part of the jigsaw, as were the other aircraft and ships of the allied Naval forces that were involved.

The Sunderland flying boats and RAF Mount Batten would become bound up in the legends of the Second World War. The involvement of the Royal Australian Air Force in the defence of the realm also contributed to this special status. Local people remembered the presence of the Australians at Mount Batten for a number of reasons; not only because of their different lingo, the shade of their blue uniforms that was darker than those of the RAF, but also the roar of the Sunderland engines when one of these flying boats took off.

The Australians maintained their fight against the German U-boats with steadfast resolve – throughout the war and until the end of hostilities. There would be no glamour attached to their war, as there was with the daring exploits of fighter pilots. The contribution of their crews, as well as their ground staff, was a daunting task of courage and devotion at Mount Batten. During the war no aircraft flew further or more often than a Sunderland. The operations involved continuous toil and monotony, in all kinds of weather over the seas on patrols that usually lasted between eight and 16 hours – sometimes longer. To sight a periscope was rare. If a submarine was sighted it would be attacked. The Australians sometimes lost aircraft on their operations. If an aircraft came down into the sea and the crew survived, it could mean hours, perhaps even days, in a life-raft, often in freezing conditions or gale-force winds, but always with the hope of being rescued; some perished, others survived. When a Sunderland

Jacques Hazard (centre) was the pilot of the Besson seaplane. He had remained at Devonport and had not sailed in the Surcouf *that was sunk in the Pacific. He was befriended by Australian airmen at Mount Batten and eventually was allowed to serve as an officer in the Royal Australian Airforce. He lost his life in June 1942 on an air-sea rescue search. His name is on the memorial at St John's Church, Hooe.*

returned at night the dark sky over Plymouth Sound would be, for a moment, lit up by rockets. Then the aircraft would descend, guided by the glow of a flare path. Night landings were potentially hazardous, even with flares, as it was difficult for the pilot to see the blacked-out ships and the surface of the water.

RAF Mount Batten gained in importance when it assumed administrative control for RAF Roborough. The air-sea rescue units at Fowey, Salcombe and Torquay were also, for a time, under the control of RAF Mount Batten.

The Legend of the *Surcouf*

One of the most remarkable aircraft associated with the wartime history of Mount Batten during the

The French-built Surcouf, *was once the largest submarine in the world. It carried a small seaplane kept in a hangar located at the rear of its conning tower. After the submarine's arrival at Devonport in 1940, it was shrouded in mystery.*

A picture of the Besson MB411 seaplane that was carried by the Surcouf *on the concourse at RAF Mount Batten, c.1941. It is recorded that the seaplane had been damaged in an air raid on Devonport and had been sent to Batten for repair.*

An historic picture taken from RAF Mount Batten, c.1941. Beyond the Sunderland flying boat is the giant battleship HMS Hood *steaming out of Plymouth Sound from Devonport. Two months after this picture was taken HMS* Hood *was blown up and sunk with the loss of most of the ship's company.*

Second World War was a French Besson MB seaplane, a waif of a plane. The Besson was used as a scout that went in search of enemy shipping. It was housed in a watertight hangar immediately aft of the conning tower (the superstructure of a submarine from which steering, firing, etc., are directed on or near the surface, and which contains the periscope) of the giant French submarine *Surcouf*, then the largest submarine in the world. The *Surcouf* had arrived at Devonport shrouded in mystery because of the suspected allegiance of some of its crew members. The seaplane would be taken from its hangar and lowered by a small crane on board into the water. The Besson had a flying range of 50 miles. On return the Besson, whose wings could be folded back, was then lifted out of the water and onto the submarine.

While at Devonport the Besson seaplane was damaged by a bomb and sent to RAF Mount Batten to be repaired. It was further damaged in April 1941, still at Mount Batten. There is an unconfirmed report that the wrecked Besson was stored in a hangar at Mount Batten for the rest of the war; what happened to it afterwards is not known.

The Besson pilot, Jacques Hazard, was not required to cross the Atlantic with the *Surcouf* in 1941. There are a number of theories about exactly what happened to the submarine, which vanished amid rumours and mystery. Explanations given for *Surcouf's* disappearance include its sinking in the

Gulf of Mexico in November 1942, its being rammed and sunk by an American freighter near the Panama Canal in February 1942, its being swallowed by the Bermuda Triangle and its sinking in Long Island Sound because it was refuelling a German U-boat.

Jacques Hazard, who had been left behind in Plymouth, was at a loss over what to do. He could not speak English but went over to Mount Batten, where he was befriended by some Australian airmen. Somehow he managed to be officially posted to No. 10 Squadron of the Royal Australian Air Force. He was to become the only Frenchman attached to the Australian Air Force during the Second World War. Hazard was a very capable pilot and became a Flying Officer. Flying from Mount Batten he was killed in action with ten other RAAF crew members while on an air-sea rescue mission. His name is commemorated on one of the memorial tablets in St John's Church, Hooe.

Mount Batten During the Early 1940s

The battle ground for Coastal Command had extended to the Bay of Biscay and the vast area of the Western Approaches. The Sunderlands watched and searched for U-boats that had surfaced. The submarines had to come to the surface at some stage in order to recharge their batteries, expel the fouled air inside the submarine and allow fresh air in. This was essential to the survival of the crew. It was a balancing act for the crew; when the submarine

A dramatic picture taken by an Australian airman from RAF Mount Batten of the centre of Plymouth on fire, on the first night of the Plymouth Blitz, 20 March 1941.

A German reconnaissance picture of part of Plymouth taken on 24 April 1941. Many readers will recognise locations around the Cattewater, including the line of oil tanks at Radford, that were supposed to have been camouflaged.

Winston Churchill and his wife seated in the rear of the saloon during their visit to Plymouth to tour the stricken city, May 1941. Although not publicised at the time, Churchill's first call on this day was to visit RAF Mount Batten to inspect the station's bomb damage.

The majestic features of the Sunderland flying boat are clearly seen in this picture. To the left is the tail end of another flying boat, where the rear gunner was placed to defend the aircraft.

The giant Berwick flying boat that brought Winston Churchill back to RAF Mount Batten from America. This was the largest flying boat ever to touch down on the waters of Plymouth Sound.

Left: *Jack Kelly-Rogers, Captain of the Berwick who at one time was stationed at RAF Mount Batten.*

Below: *Winston Churchill smoking a huge cigar at the controls of the Berwick while flying across the Atlantic to land at Plymouth, 1942.*

Above: *Winston Churchill wearing his famous siren suit on the flight deck of the Berwick that landed in Plymouth Sound, having secretly flown across the Atlantic Ocean.*

A Sunderland of RAAF No. 10 Squadron on the edge of the slipway at Mount Batten being brought in for servicing. There must have been at least 30 ground crew in attendance. The aircraft was shot down over the Bay of Biscay with the loss of its crew on 17 May 1943.

Left: *This Sunderland L2163 was flown by 10 Squadron RAAF at Mount Batten. It was sunk at Stranraer in a gale in 1942 but recovered for further service.*

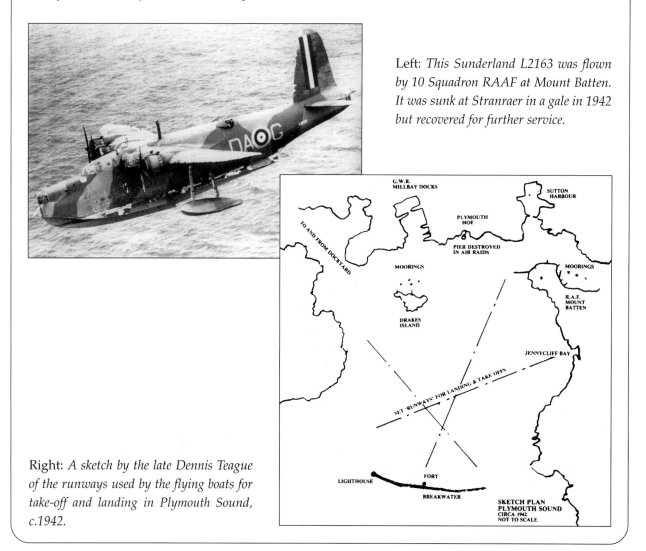

Right: *A sketch by the late Dennis Teague of the runways used by the flying boats for take-off and landing in Plymouth Sound, c.1942.*

A member of the Women's Auxiliary Air Force sitting on a bollard on the Mount Batten Breakwater, taking time off to do some knitting, then a popular and relaxing occupation.

During the Second World War, pigeons were carried by aircrew on operational flights in case of emergencies. This picture is of the wartime pigeon loft at RAF Mount Batten.

Inside the pigeon loft at RAF Mount Batten showing the pigeon holes. At Mount Batten the pigeons were trained to carry messages.

A blue checker cock pigeon which returned to RAF Mount Batten with an SOS message from a ditched Sunderland aircraft of No. 10 Squadron RAAF on 16 September 1944.

surfaced it became a target, but when it submerged it used up its power.

Since June 1940, enemy submarines were using the French Atlantic Naval bases. The Sunderland aircraft also had to contend with enemy aircraft flying from occupied French airfields on France's northwest coast. This meant that allied shipping was more open to attack by U-boats and enemy aircraft.

The air attacks on Plymouth and the mines that had been laid in the vicinity meant that the Cattewater and Plymouth Sound had become an unsafe arena in which the Australian Sunderland aircraft could operate. The decision was therefore taken to relocate No. 10 RAAF Squadron from Mount Batten to Pembroke Dock, South Wales.

(Sir) John Colville, Private Secretary to Winston Churchill, records in his diary that on 2 May 1941 Winston Churchill visited RAF Mount Batten to inspect the bomb damage caused in April's Plymouth Blitz. He then proceeded by launch to Devonport Dockyard and a tour of the bombed city.

On 11 May 1941 three Short S.26 class flying boats arrived at Mount Batten. These had been built for Imperial Airways in 1938 for air-mail service and to fly passengers in luxury across the Atlantic. The three giant flying boats named *Golden Hind, Golden Fleece* and *Golden Horn* had been impressed to serve the RAF. For a short while they were attached to No. 10 Squadron RAAF for special flights to Gibraltar and the Middle East. An unsuccessful search was made on 21 June 1941 for the *Golden Fleece* that was lost during a flight from Mount Batten to Gibraltar. In December of that year the two remaining flying boats were returned to the British Overseas Corporation and restored to civilian use to fly priority passengers from Poole to various overseas venues. Early in 1942 the Sunderlands of No. 10 Squadron of the RAAF returned to Mount Batten from Pembroke.

Even in wartime it must have been a marvellous sight to watch the largest flying boat in the world, a Boeing 314, the Berwick, descend and touch down on the waters of Plymouth Sound. The plane did just that on 17 January 1942 after completing a secret flight of 3,365 miles from Bermuda. On board was Winston Churchill and members of his Cabinet as well as senior members of the Armed Services who had attended a conference with President Roosevelt in Washington. They had arrived in America travelling on the battleship HMS *Duke of York*. After the conference the Prime Minister and his officials travelled by train to Norfolk, Virginia, and then flew in

the Berwick, commanded by Captain Kelly Rogers, to Bermuda. Mr Churchill spoke at a secret meeting with his ministers stating:

... outside lies the Duke of York *waiting to take me to England which I can reach in seven to nine days. During that time I have ears but no lips with which to speak. On the other hand, Captain Kelly Rogers assures me that in the aeroplane in which we have flown to Bermuda today we can fly to England tomorrow in not more than 22 hours. This is many days saved and during that time many things may happen. Two important battles may be fought and one major decision...*

Weather permitting Churchill decided he would travel by air with seven passengers; a start would be made the following morning. This would be the first flight a British Prime Minister – indeed any leader of any nation – would make across the Atlantic.

To maintain secrecy the flight course was set to fly from Bermuda to Pembroke Dock without the aid of radio communications, to prevent enemy interception. As dawn broke Kelly Rogers began his descent approaching Land's End. The weather was changing, visibility at Pembroke Dock stood at only 500 yards. It was decided to change course and fly to Plymouth, where the weather was better, although there was fog. Looking down Captain Rogers could see the coast, then the Mewstone through the fog, Staddon Heights and Mount Batten. The Berwick circled the Sound and the final descent was made by Captain Shakespeare. He lost horizontal visibility and climbed and circled again before making his descent with Drake's Island visible ahead. He crossed the Plymouth Breakwater at a height of 50 feet.

The Berwick touched down on Plymouth Sound one minute ahead of schedule, after a crossing of 17 hours 55 minutes. The great war leader's first Atlantic crossing thus became part of the history of Mount Batten. Next day Captain Rogers was invited to join a family reunion luncheon at No. 10 Downing Street in order that Mrs Churchill might express to him her thanks for having carried her husband safely back to her.

There is an interesting link to the past regarding Captain Kelly Rogers and RAF Mount Batten. Rogers was stationed there in the early 1930s at the time of T.E. Lawrence was there. Both were part of the same crew that delivered an RAF motor launch to Donibristle, Scotland. Furthermore Kelly Rogers was

A Consolidated Catalina of the RAAF. Only a few Catalinas were based at Mount Batten during the war, including those flown by the Royal Canadian Air Force.

one of the men who was with Lawrence out in Plymouth Sound searching for survivors after the 1931 flying boat disaster.

Early in May 1942 a Sunderland piloted by Flight Lieutenant Tom Stokes had flown from Plymouth to Gibraltar to collect Lord Gort, VC, to fly him to Malta. Lord Gort had recently been appointed Governor of Malta by Winston Churchill. The importance of the journey was enhanced as inside Lord Gort's attaché case was Malta's George Cross medal, uniquely awarded to the people of the island by King George VI.

At home there was enemy action around Mount Batten when on 16 May 1942, the central barrage balloon on Plymouth Breakwater was shot down in flames by enemy fighters that appeared undetected by flying in at almost sea level. Six days later RAF Mount Batten was warned to expect low-flying attacks by fighter aircraft, this resulted in No. 10 Squadron's Sunderlands being dispersed around the moorings in Plymouth Sound and on the Hamoaze.

The number of U-boats operating in the Bay of Biscay area was of grave concern to Coastal Command; although anti-submarine patrols were maintained, there were nevertheless reports of the damage or sinking by enemy submarines. A new Australian flying boat No. 461 Squadron was formed at Mount Batten in April 1942, becoming operational

in July of that year. Unfortunately its Commanding Officer, Wing Commander Haliday, lost his life while attempting an air-sea rescue of a ditched aircraft. This resulted in an order being issued forbidding flying boats to descend onto the water to rescue survivors (this order was often ignored by the Australian aircrews). The death of Wing Commander Haliday was followed two days later by the loss of a Mount Batten Sunderland shot down by enemy aircraft. No. 461 Squadron was moved from Mount Batten to Hamworthy in August 1942.

An important yet relatively unknown operational component involving Coastal Command at Mount Batten was the use of pigeons. They were kept in a large pigeon loft that was sited on the hillside at the back of the camp. The Australians (similar to other service units) used these birds as message carriers because of their remarkable homing instincts. Preparing for an operational flight a crew member would take a pigeon in a wicker carrier basket on board the aircraft. If for some reason the aircraft ditched in the sea the pigeon would be released with a message referring to the survivors' bearing, and hopefully make its way back to base. Such a feat was demonstrated on 21 May 1942, when a Plymouth-bred and trained pigeon was released from a Sunderland flying boat in the Atlantic, 120 miles from its base at

A Sunderland flying boat of the Royal Australian Air Force, taking off from Plymouth Sound for an operational mission over the Atlantic, c.1943.

Personnel from No. 10 Squadron RAAF having marched from RAF Mount Batten, through Hooe, on a 'Wings for Victory Parade'. Here they are taking the salute at Plymstock on 15 May 1943.

Above: *A head-on picture of ground crew, working together to haul a Sunderland aircraft up onto the slipway in May 1945. Many of the Australian airmen wore berets when working.*

R. A. F.   R. A. A. F.

MOUNT BATTEN

Christmas 1943

BREAKFAST

CEREAL
BACON AND EGG   CHIPOLATA
TEA   COFFEE   ROLLS   BUTTER   SAUSAGE   MARMALADE

DINNER

SCOTCH BROTH
ROAST TURKEY   ROAST PORK
FORCEMEAT BALLS   APPLE SAUCE   STUFFING
ROAST POTATOES   POMME DUCHESSE
BRUSSEL SPROUTS   GRAVY
CHRISTMAS PUDDING   CUSTARD SAUCE
MINCE PIES
CHEESE AND BISCUITS
BEER   MINERALS   CIGARETTES
FRUIT

TEA

BRISKET OF BEEF
POTATO   SALAD   PICKLES
TEA   BREAD   MARGARINE   JAM
FRUIT CAKE   MINCE PIES

The Christmas menu for the RAF and RAAF, 1943.

A picture taken through the geometric-patterned scaffolding of a RAAF Sunderland flying boat outside a hangar at RAF Mount Batten.

WAAF engine flight mechanics supervised by an NCO fitter servicing a starboard engine at RAF Mount Batten, 1943.

Ground staff servicing the four powerful engines of a Sunderland flying boat, working on specially constructed platforms. To the right of the picture the single-storey building was used as the officers' mess during the First World War.

A Sunderland flying boat that had been blown on to the rocks at Jennycliff after a ship had sailed too close to the aircraft and cut the mooring ropes on 2 April 1944.

Happiness in wartime. The wedding of Sergeant W. Leggate of No. 10 Squadron of Melbourne and Leading Aircraftwoman P. Williams from Paignton. The wedding took place at St John's Church, Hooe, on 4 September 1943.

The German hospital ship Rostock, *flying a swastika at anchor in Bovisand Bay during September 1944, after being intercepted at sea by a Sunderland flying boat of No. 10 Squadron RAAF. The* Rostock *had been escorted into Plymouth Sound by two Royal Navy torpedo boats and the destroyer HMS* Urania.

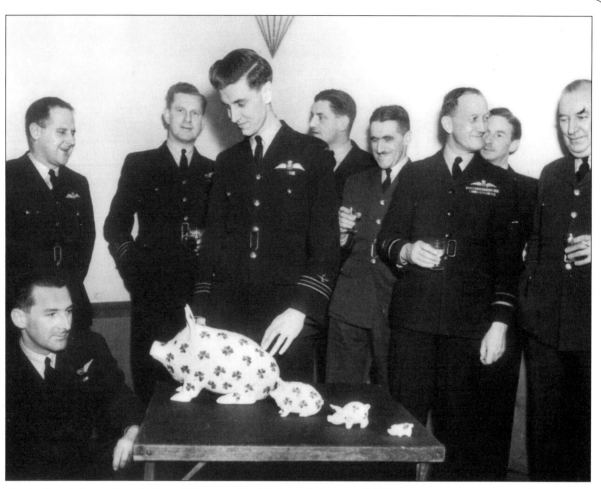

Senior Royal Australian Airforce Officers and RAF Coastal Command Officers at a reception in the officers' mess, Mount Batten. A RAAF Squadron Leader arranges the famous spotted pigs that were No. 10 Squadron RAAF mascots.

Christmas dinner at the airmen's mess, RAF Mount Batten, 25 December 1944.

There were five generations of Sunderland military flying boats – this one of No. 10 Squadron RAAF, flying along the South West coast, was a Mark V. On 12 October 1944 this Mount Batten aircraft sank at its moorings.

Mount Batten. The bird flew home and delivered its message within 145 minutes.

Among the aircraft that were based at Mount Batten was the Consolidated Catalina flying boat flown by the RAAF and Royal Canadian Air Force. The Catalina was one of the most successful flying boats in aviation history; its capabilities included long-range reconnaissance, convoy protection and air-sea rescue. One feature of its design was its stabilising floats that retracted in flight to form the wing tips. There were at least two Catalina aircraft based at Mount Batten. The operational records of RAF Mount Batten record that these seaplanes would fly to Gibraltar. Other seaplanes associated with RAF Mount Batten during the war included the Fairey Swordfish, known as a 'stringbag' (because of its brace wires), the Fairey Sea Fox and the Kingfisher. The Swordfish was used throughout the war, and was the last biplane to see active service.

The War Progresses

The year 1943 was to be an important year of operations concerning the Battle of the Atlantic; not only were there more enemy submarines, but the Germans and Italians had introduced an important change in tactics. Instead of diving on receiving a warning of an allied aircraft in the vicinity, now the U-boats remained on the surface and fought out the battle with anti-aircraft guns that had been installed on the U-boats. Furthermore, enemy aircraft patrolled in groups of up to eight aircraft. Coastal Command was

having to use cover to protect their aircraft by using Beaufighter and Mosquito fighter planes.

The enemy, however, were wary of attacking a Sunderland flying boat, which they called 'Flying Porcupines'. This name came about because some of the five types of Sunderland flying boats had four ventrical receiving masts on top of the rear fuselage, which gave the craft a spiky look. However, it was the Sunderland's fire-power that gave the enemy cause for concern; near the end of the war these flying boats were equipped with at least 16 machine-guns.

The success of the Mount Batten aircrews were dependant on the technical skills of the ground crews. As the war proceeded these men worked up to 11 hours a day, sometimes more. At RAF Mount Batten, Australian and British airmen worked together. Also working alongside the men were contingents of WAAFS (Women's Auxiliary Air Force) who performed a variety of tasks, including technical maintenance work on the aircraft. These young women were billeted at Mount Batten, and a small number of women were known to be billeted with families at Hooe.

Before an aircrew set off on its operational mission, a sequence of events would have been started: the operation list would be displayed on the noticeboard and aircrew would check to see if their names were on the list. Wearing their flying gear, the men collected their food rations and reported to the operation room. Here a map hung on the wall, showing arrows to signify ships and the course they were to

Landing craft assembled in Plymouth in preparation for D Day in May 1944. Mount Batten can be seen in the background with Sunderland flying boats in the Cattewater. The concentration of craft made it difficult for the pilots of the flying boats to take off and land.

take. Other markers related to enemy aircraft, U-boats and warships. In the briefing, matters relating to intelligence, signals and the weather forecast would be discussed. The aircrew would then be ferried to their aircraft in the Cattewater. People standing on Plymouth Hoe would watch as they heard the giant flying boats' engines increase their power to accelerate. As the crafts moved across the water they produced a spray like a giant flying fish. Eventually they pulled away from the sea, becoming airborne and flying off. People watched as the planes disappeared into the distant horizon, the onlookers not knowing the purpose of the flight or the fate of the crew and the aircraft.

Throughout the war there were several changes within the camp. The flying boat station was equipped with its own cinema and, with the extra number of men stationed at Mount Batten, the canteen for the ranks was extended. Leave would be taken and airmen would make their way over to

Plymouth for their entertainment. The Australians stationed at mount Batten proved very popular with the local girls. Some men would go seeking out relatives, as many Plymouthians emigrated to Australia during the eighteenth and nineteenth centuries. Other airmen went to the nearby villages to drink. On Sunday airmen would worship at one of the local villages.

In 1943 the casualties mounted and the Mount Batten Australians lost eight Sunderlands through enemy action, which amounted to over 100 men. As was the usual procedure in war, when one crew went missing (which could mean the loss of 13 men), the pragmatic approach had to be that another crew simply took its place. To make matters worse aircraft continued to be destroyed by accident. For example, a Sunderland that suffered engine failure came down in Plymouth Sound and sank; two of its crew were killed. Worse was to follow when seven civilians and two airmen of a salvage crew that went out to the stricken aircraft were killed when it is believed the depth charges in the aircraft exploded. One factor that contributed to the accidents that occurred in the home waters was the restriction of lights and the high density of shipping in Plymouth Sound – both factors made the descent difficult. Yet despite all this, the allies were beginning to win the war against the marauding U-boats, even though it was doing so with mounting losses of Coastal Command aircraft.

A Turning Point: D Day

The preparation of the allied invasion of Europe added another dimension to the operations of Coastal Command. The operation led to intensive searching for the enemy, so as to protect the shipping that was carrying troops and vast quantities of arms from America. Plymouth was an important pre-invasion port. There was a large American presence in and around Plymouth and they brought with them their own seaplanes that included the Duck, Seagull, and Seamew. Here at Plymouth, amphibious craft assembled to carry American troops and equipment for exercises at Slapton Sands and other nearby beaches. As D Day approached the concentration of craft space severely restricted the movement of flying

boats; it seemed at times that flying was impossible.

In September 1944, a Sunderland severed its mooring and was driven onto the rocks at Jennycliff and was seen to break up in front of RAF Mount Batten's officers' mess, which faced out to Plymouth Sound.

The War is Over

With the ending of the war No. 10 Squadron of the Royal Australian Airforce was disbanded and the airman warriors departed from Mount Batten for home. The Australians went, leaving some of their dead to rest in peace at St John's Church, Hooe, or at Efford cemetery in Plymouth. At St John's there are two rolls of honour commemorating the members of the Royal Australian Air Force and Royal Air Force who died on active service while at RAF Mount Batten. Some 20 years later a plaque depicting a Sunderland flying boat was flown over from Australia and unveiled at a ceremony held at Plymouth. It is inscribed, 'To the people of Plymouth with affection and admiration from the members of No. 10 Squadron, Royal Australian Air Force who operated from Mount Batten 1939–1945. The plaque is set in a wall at the bottom of Lambhay Hill, overlooking the Barbican.

The badge of RAAF No. 10 Squadron depicting an Atlantic Chimera pierced by an Australian aboriginal fishing spear, with the motto Strike First.

HMAFV Spitfire with Mount Batten in the background, c.1980.

Remembering the Civil War conflict beside the memorial stone (foreground, right). During the seventeenth century a battle took place at Mount Batten in the vicinity of where St Luke's Hospice now stands. The picture also gives a glimpse of some of the houses of the new community at Mount Batten to the right of the picture.

The Postwar Years and Regeneration

Mount Batten made national headline news when on 23 March 1955 the Norwegian liner *Venus* anchored off Jennycliff Bay was driven ashore by a gale-force wind, onto the rocks in front of the airmen's barracks. Rocket lines were used to rig breech boys to rescue 105 members of the crew. The ship was eventually refloated and sent to Devonport for repairs. This was the last time the Mount Batten auxiliary coastguard used its rocket apparatus. The British Empire Medal was awarded to Mr R. Demellweek for his part in the rescue.

After the Australian airmen had left Mount Batten, a maintenance unit arrived with responsibility for keeping the station on a reserve footing to allow Sunderland flying boats from Pembroke and Poole to call there, this facility continued until 1958.

The flying boat had performed a wonderful service throughout the war. However, the design and performance of land-based aircraft had made rapid advances as had systems of communication, making the flying boat obsolete as a weapon of war. Despite this, Mount Batten still had an important contribution to make for the RAF when the marine craft training school was transferred to Plymouth from Calshot. Eventually Mount Batten became the principal station of the RAF Marine Craft unit resulting in a number of different air-sea rescue craft being based in the Cattewater, where once the flying boats were tethered. The aircraft hangars and slipways

were used for craft maintenance and training. Mount Batten became multifunctional as it was selected for the headquarters of the Commander Maritime Air sub area, part of the North Atlantic Treaty Organisation.

The RAF Marine Branch had been formed in April 1918, just a few days after the Royal Air Force was established, when there was no air-sea rescue. The crafts were then used to service the RAF seaplanes and patrol the landing paths. Since the First World War, RAF marine craft were built based on an Admiralty specification. Some boats needed a fire to be lit in order to heat the boiler to produce sufficient steam to get the craft to start – in effect, these boats lacked power and speed. It was here in Plymouth in the early 1930s that the concept of a dedicated air-sea rescue service had its origins. T.E. Lawrence, when stationed at Mount Batten, had advocated the need for a powerful rescue craft for the Royal Air Force following the tragic accident in 1931 when a Blackburn Iris flying boat crashed into Plymouth Sound (outlined in Chapter 3). Consequently a powerboat was built at Hythe and

The liner Venus *on the rocks off Mount Batten having dragged her anchor during the storm of 23 March 1955. The stricken ship was illuminated by searchlights from RAF Mount Batten. Crowds of people watched the scene from Jennycliff.*

No. 1380 was a 63-foot service pinnace shown in the picture participating in exercises involving the RAF School of Survival, based at Mount Batten. This picture was taken off Rame Head, Cornwall, c.1980.

Entering RAF Mount Batten meant reporting to the guard room (left) *then travelling along Lawrence Road passing the airmen's married quarters. This photograph was taken on 8 July 1984.*

trials of the prototype RAF 200 were held in Plymouth Sound and out in the English Channel. This boat was to remain in service for the next 50 years and was involved in operations on such crucial occasions as Dunkirk, the Battle of Britain and D Day. During the war the Air Sea Rescue Service was introduced and is credited with saving 13,000 lives.

The RAF 200 craft had, over the years, been subjected to a series of modifications, but even this gallant boat needed to be replaced as faster seagoing vessels for search and rescue were required. After the war, King George VI had granted royal approval for a new seagoing marine craft to be designated His Majesty's Air Force Vessel (HMAFV). RAF Marine craft were now larger and more powerful. A school of survival had been established in 1959 at Mount Batten where all aircrews had to attend a training course each year. This included being ditched at sea, to perform dinghy and life-raft drill. The skills used in air-sea rescue were then consolidated by using powerboats cooperating with helicopters. This eventually led to the marine craft being replaced completely by air-sea rescue helicopters.

The end of an Era

The Air Ministry decided the Royal Air Force Marine Branch would be disbanded after serving the RAF for 68 years. On 8 January 1986, a ceremony was held at Mount Batten to officially close down the RAF Marine Branch. At the public ceremony the RAF Marine Craft Section ensign was lowered for the last time.

In 1987 another important part of Mount Batten's function came to an end with the transfer of the Mount Batten weather centre to St Mawgan, West Cornwall. Opened in 1920, the prime function for the first 30 years of its operation was to supply the locally based service units with weather reports. During the Second World War forecasts were supplied not only to RAF Mount Batten but other bases, including the fighter station at Harrowbeer and RAF Davidstow, North Cornwall. After the war the weather station supplied forecasts to the public sector. In 1991 the station was moved back to Derry's Cross, Plymouth.

The Air Ministry issued a statement in 1989 that Mount Batten was no longer financially viable and would close within the next three–four years. In 1992

Lowering the RAF Marine Craft Section Ensign on the ceremonial disbandment of the RAF Marine Branch, Mount Batten, on 8 January 1986.

A CEREMONY TO MARK THE DISBANDMENT OF THE ROYAL AIR FORCE MARINE BRANCH

Held at RAF Mount Batten, Plymouth
on Wednesday, 8th January, 1986

TIMETABLE OF EVENTS

1430 hours	Spectators to be seated.
1445 hours	The Western Band of the Royal Air Force plays incidental music.
1450 hours	Air Officers arrive.
1455 hours	The Queen's Colour Squadron of the Royal Air Force Regiment march on followed by the Band.
1500 hours	Arrival of Chief of the Air Staff. General Salute. Inspection of the Guard of Honour.
1507 hours	Address by the Chief of the Air Staff.
1512 hours	The Director of Royal Air Force Marine Craft presents a marine craft bell into the care and safekeeping of the Central Church of the Royal Air Force; received by the Resident Chaplain of St Clement Danes. (Gentlemen should remove their hats when prayers are said at this time)
1515 hours	Display by the Colour Squadron and Band.
1540 hours	Sunset Ceremony; ensign lowered.
1545 hours	Ceremony ends.
1700 hours	Event Terminated.

Programme of events for the disbandment of the RAF Marine Branch in 1986.

an official announcement was made that RAF Mount Batten was to permanently close down. To mark this historic occasion three successive days of pomp and circumstance ceremonies were held. This started when the last officers 'dining in night' took place at the officers' mess on Friday 3 July 1992. The guests, many of them in their splendid dress uniform, included men who had served at Mount Batten back in the early 1930s with No. 204 Squadron. Also present were men who had travelled from Australia, having served with No. 10 Squadron of the Royal Australian Air Force stationed at Mount Batten. The guests arrived by car or limousine at the pillared portico entrance of the officers' mess and were met by an RAF officer who ushered them into the grand reception room. The VIPs present included the Lord Mayor and Lady Mayoress of Plymouth, Lord Morley and Air Marshal Sir John Harris. After sherry the guests went out to view the Beating of the Retreat. The guests then made their way to the

magnificent dining-hall where the silver service and candelabra were displayed on highly polished wooden tables.

The officers' mess and the hall were covered with paintings and photographs recording the station's years of history. One portrait that hung in a central position was that of T.E. Lawrence, drawn by artist Eric Kennington. This was remarkable, for here was the portrait of an RAF ranker hanging in the 'inner sanctum' of an officers' mess. There were speeches and a magnificent dinner, throughout which the wine flowed. For those who attended, this was an evening they would never forget.

The following day more than 500 people gathered at Mount Batten in warm sunny weather to attend the Closing Down Parade. Guests enjoyed the sound of the bagpipes and watched the marching, before the formal ceremonies of the salute and inspection of the Guard of Honour. This preceded the solemn lowering of the RAF ensign and a speech by Air Marshall Sir John Harris that signified the end of the

PLYMOUTH LOCAL NOTICE TO MARINERS 2/86

VISIT OF CATALINA FLYING BOATS TO PLYMOUTH 31st MAY, 1986

1. In order to commemorate the arrival on 31st May, 1919 of the first flying boat to cross the Atlantic and the 75th Anniversary of US Naval Aviation, two Catalina flying boats will follow the original itinerary and arrive in Plymouth Sound at 1100 on Saturday, 31st May, 1986.

2. A runway (A, B or C on the attached diagram) will be selected dependent on wind direction and will be cleared by QHM's craft and Police boats. These craft will show a red flag whilst clearing the area and a green flag when the aircraft is clear to touch down. After landing the Catalinas will taxi to moorings off RAF Mountbatten (M1 and M2) and disembark passengers for a Civic Reception. They will depart Mountbatten at 1700 for a cleared runway in the vicinity of B and C.

3. All ships and craft are to keep at least 200 metres clear of the runways while the Runway Clearance Craft are showing red or green flags. Despite the provisions of the rule of the road, all underway craft are to keep 200 metres clear ahead and 100 metres clear astern of the Catalinas while they are taxiing. Catalinas have **NO** astern power.

8th May, 1986

W. H. H. McLEOD
Captain, Royal Navy
Queen's Harbourmaster

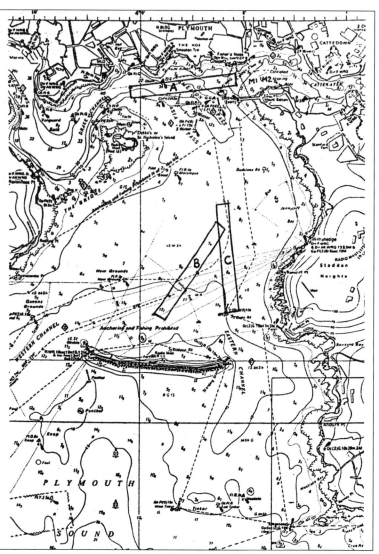

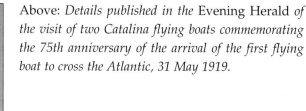

Above: *Details published in the* Evening Herald *of the visit of two Catalina flying boats commemorating the 75th anniversary of the arrival of the first flying boat to cross the Atlantic, 31 May 1919.*

Left: *The imposing front entrance to the officers' mess just before it was demolished. Left to right: Mrs Joan Jago (wife of Darell Jago, aviation historian), the late Dennis Teague (aviation historian), Mrs Betty Teague.*

The scene of the closing parade at RAF Mount Batten that took place outside the 'Sunderland' hangar in the presence of 500 visitors on 4 July 1992.

remarkable aviation presence at Mount Batten. Later a reception was held in the 'Sunderland Hangar' before the guests and spectators departed. The three days of commemoration ended at Mount Batten with a service of thanksgiving on the Sunday morning of 5 July 1992 that was conducted by three chaplains of the Royal Air Force.

Decisions About the Future

In the coming weeks RAF personnel and civilian employees were transferred or left the service. Local people were concerned about what would happen to Mount Batten as Plymouth City Council, the major beneficiary, had no direct authority over the initial changes in the landfall. There had, prior to the offi-

cial announcement of closure, been proposals of how the land at Mount Batten should be used. Lord David Owen had written to the Secretary of State for Defence requesting the Ministry of Defence release RAF Mount Batten for use as a water sports centre. In 1989 proposals for the future use of Mount Batten included letters from Professor B. Cuncliffe of the Institute of Archaeology concerning the need to preserve RAF Mount Batten as it is a historically important site. During this interim period one of the hangars was used by the BBC as a depot for props and the huge number of costumes worn by the cast who were filming Jane Austin's *Sense and Sensibility* at Saltram House.

In 1994 the future of the 77 acres once occupied by RAF Mount Batten's flying boat station was decided

Terry Hugo at the closing parade at RAF Mount Batten, 4 July 1992, next to Mary Antony, who made an important contribution to recording the history of the RAF station and the Red Funnel ferry service. Mary's friend sits alongside.

Terry Hugo at RAF Mount Batten with the team of Oxford University archaeologists who were involved in the excavations at Mount Batten, c.1983–85.

when the Ministry of Defence sold its land at Mount Batten to the Plymouth Development Corporation (PDC), a quango set up in 1993, that had received £40 million from the Government and European Union to invest in local community and regeneration projects. Of this money, £11.4 million would be spent by the PDC on Mount Batten.

The first step had been taken to open part of Mount Batten the public. The PDC had drawn up various options as to how the site would develop. There were hopes that a shipyard would open to build wooden fishing craft, once a common industry in the West Country. Reports indicated that the National Maritime Museum was interested in coming to Mount Batten. A suggestion was even made that a space centre should be built at Mount Batten. The City Council had hopes that an interpretation centre would be established at Mount Batten to explain the area's interesting history to the tens of thousands of visitors that were expected to visit the place every year.

After surveys had been conducted, there were consultations and decision making before the practical work of demolition and construction started. Early work included refurbishing the sea wall and reinforcing the Mount Batten's Breakwater by depositing boulders around the structure as a protection against the sea. The rocks around Mount Batten are now protected by international law to help ensure the survival of marine life.

Many of the old military buildings were demolished, although the ancient round tower, designated a Grade II listed monument was left to stand on the rock, to continue to dominate the surrounding area. Its survival so far is due to the generosity of public-spirited people who in 1962 raised sufficient money to prevent its threatened demolition. The giant aircraft hangars are also designated Grade II listed monuments. These are fine examples of original hangars for flying boats and were in use during two world wars and were very much a part of the country's fight for survival. Furthermore, they are part of the history of aviation in this country. The hangars are now used by commercial marine companies to repair and refurbish seagoing craft.

The two original large flying boat hangars built in the First World War at Mount Batten have not changed in appearance. In 2006 they house yachts and other marine craft to be repaired or refurbished.

The seaplanes have long gone, as has the RAF station. Everything has changed except the view from Mount Batten that is essentially the same.

Yachts and powerboats in action almost within the shadows of the ancient round tower.

A Life of Leisure

The Mount Batten Centre offers a variety of activities that includes learning or improving sailing skills. Close to the entrance of the watersports centre once stood the Victorian public house, The Castle Inn that later became the official residence of the station's Commanding Officer, a place Lawrence of Arabia frequented when he was stationed there to socialise with Wing Commander Sydney Smith and his wife. Many years later this building was demolished and replaced with a brick-built sergeants' mess.

The fish factory, possibly the oldest building on Mount Batten, except for the round tower, has been refurbished and opened up as a hotel and public house. The Breakwater Arms, once home to the weather station (which later was moved on to the hillside) and the station's photographic unit is now a restaurant.

Anglers come to fish from the Breakwater, others to take in the view; the scene from the promenade is spectacular. Henry Elford, the owner of the Victorian steam ferries that gracefully ploughed through the Cattewater would have been pleased to see a ferry now calls at Mount Batten again.

Whatever the changes that have taken place at Mount Batten perhaps the most significant is the residential development of houses to the east of the peninsula. The house owners who live on this land have inherited, like the Cattewater villages, a most fascinating local history of war and peace.

Left: *On top of Mount Batten's quarry by the ancient round tower. People, and there were many more gathered for the unveiling of the tablet, were present to commemorate the presence of No. 204 Squadron RAF, 10 September 1992.*

The public walk along the Mount Batten Breakwater, c.2004, where once seaplanes were hauled from the water by a crane and placed in a row by the side of the wall. A row of modern terraced houses built on Mount Batten can be seen in the background.

Chapter 7

The Cattewater Villages

The small riverside villages situated close to Mount Batten were at one time part of a rural haven of inland hills covered in green pastures and wooded areas that border on the fertile soil of the South Hams. The land has been cultivated for generations, but the farms that are still worked are no longer a major source of employment for the local people, furthermore farm land has been built on for housing. The three villages Hooe, Turnchapel and Oreston, have aspects of their histories that are shared by Mount Batten. All are associated with quarrying, shipbuilding and have a history of being involved in military conflict. The communities are in the parish of Plymstock and with Mount Batten are part of the city of Plymouth. Most of the residents tend not to feel they are Plymouthians as their spirit of allegiance is with the smaller community in which they live. There are still residents, now in the minority, whose families have lived in one of the villages for generations, but the traditional stock of native village families in all three communities has waned over the years as descendants have died or moved out of the area, replaced by newcomers, many of whom take an active interest in their local community.

The Cattewater: A Brief History

The Cattewater, at one time spelt Catwater, is the estuary of the River Plym, that flows down from Dartmoor. It has been a safe haven for seaman through the centuries. The origin of the name is still in dispute. Crispin Gill, the eminent local Plymouth historian, records that the name could have originated from seamen who noticed a rock on the northern shore of the river shaped like a cat, that they called Cat Rock. An ancient record of 1281 refers to seamen drowning in 'apud the Catte'. In more recent times the academic Lawrence of Arabia, when he was stationed at Mount Batten, preferred to keep the name (RAF) Cattewater, because of the Danish origin of the name, rather than change it to RAF Mount Batten. He did not get his way!

During the medieval period ships were able to sail up the River Plym to Plymstock and Plympton, the silting up of the river (caused by mud and the work of the Dartmoor tinners further upstream) made the passage of seagoing vessels up the river prohibitive. The Cattewater was used as an anchorage for ships' cargoes to be unloaded and conveyed by barge to nearby Sutton Harbour. In 1671, King James II arrived at Plymouth to visit the newly built Citadel. The next day he sailed up the River Tamar as far as Saltash. On returning he visited the Cattewater, at a time when the area was involved in shipbuilding. Gill records that men working on constructing the ships at Turnchapel in the latter years of the seventeenth century lived with their families in a hulk in the Cattewater that was anchored there for nearly 40 years. Life on the hulk was not pleasant and later requests were made by the men to be offered houses, near where they worked.

Records indicate at the end of the seventeenth century the South West of England experienced considerable stormy weather. A consequence of this was that ships sought shelter in Plymouth Sound. Even so, this did not make them immune to the force of the fierce gales; vessels were dashed onto the rocks near the Citadel, close to the Cattewater. On Christmas Day, 1689, a violent storm forced the frigate HMS *Henrietta* from her anchorage in the Sound onto the rocks of Fisher's Nose under the Citadel. The storm then drove the ship into the Cattewater where she sunk. While the *Henrietta* was being battered, *Unity* a Dutch man of war was forced from her anchorage by the terrible weather and crashed into the frigate HMS *Centurion*. Both were driven ashore under Mount Batten, resulting in the *Unity* losing 150 of her crew and the *Centurion* a dozen men.

The Battle of Bantry Bay in 1689 had shown that Portsmouth was too far up the English Channel to be the dock of choice for emergency warship repair. For this reason a search began for a new docking area further west. The choice was between Dartmouth and Plymouth. The Admiralty asked its Plymouth agent if a dock could be built there. Sir John Berry visited the South West of England in search of a suitable shipyard site and reported in favour of

A view of Hooe against a rural setting, c.1920s. The Royal Oak is still in the village, but the building with the bold sign has long been demolished. This was the time when Hooe Lake was used as a place to season timber, which was then made into rafts.

A pre-First World War snapshot taken at the side of Radford Lake.

Turnchapel. However, Sir John could not find a suitable builder. At the time, Naval construction took place in the Cattewater.

In 1687 HMS *The Assistance*, having lost its foremast through bad weather, came to the Cattewater to be repaired. The area for working was cramped and would be expensive to develop as a large Naval shipyard. In 1690 the Navy Board persuaded the Admiralty to accept the Cattewater as a dockyard base, but by the following November the Board had changed its mind as it was agreed that the Hamoaze was the more substantial base for a dockyard to be built.

Storms prevailed in the South West. One gale blew into the Cattewater damaging two French prizes, other merchant ships were also damaged and cast from their moorings. The weather was not the only reason for the loss of ships in the Cattewater. The *London Gazette* records the loss of the *Mermayd*, a fireship, on 24 February 1692 as she lay at her graving place in the Cattewater. A boy had dropped a candle among some wood shavings that set the ship on fire. The blaze could not be extinguished and was simply allowed to burn.

Lord Boringdon who lived at nearby Saltram, who was to become the first Earl Morley, had been developing property at Turnchapel for shipbuilding. He laid ship moorings in the Cattewater to enable merchant ships to tie up and allow their cargoes to be transferred to Turnchapel. There were influential people including the Duchy, who argued that this would take trade away from Sutton Harbour. As a result the Admiralty made Lord Boringdon re-site his moorings.

In 1803 with England at war with France, the Cattewater in June of that year was described as 'quite a wood of French prizes', their cargoes worth £1½ million.

In 1879, across at Plymouth, the railway came to Cattedown. Then in 1890 the Cattedown Wharfs were opened but the Cattewater continued to handle more ships than Sutton Harbour. At the end of the nineteenth century only five per cent of the vessels around Plymouth were steamships and most of these were the large ocean-going liners that called at Plymouth. All the others were sailing ships or barges, mainly exporting china clay and importing petrol. However, times were changing with the increase in size of merchant ships and Millbay, Plymouth, became the dominant dock. With the coming of the First World War trading slumped and did not revive until the middle of the 1920s.

The Village of Hooe

The name Hooe is said to have been derived from the word Howe, meaning a high place. Although most of the countryside around the village is hilly, much of the community of Hooe at one time lived on flat land at water-level. Hooe has an ancient history that can be traced back to the Norman Conquest; the settlement is mentioned in the Domesday Book. Once a Saxon manor it was broken up to form three manors: Radford, East Hooe (Higher Hooe) and Lower Hooe (West Hooe). The historian Arthur Norman refers to a mill in East Hooe in 1331.

Hooe Lake

Lower Hooe is where the waterside village developed alongside the tidal Hooe Lake that is fed by the waters of the River Plym. The placid waters of Hooe Lake once offered ships shelter from the aggressive elements of the weather and was a place for trading and victualling. Later, however, the lake became silted up, and ended up being a place for abandoned hulks to gradually disintegrate. It has been known for people to moor their houseboats on the lake and live there.

Hooe Road is of particular importance as it is the main access route into the village of Turnchapel and Mount Batten. Unlike Turnchapel, a compact village, Hooe is rather spread out and extends to the boundary of Plymstock. The local countryside was once an idyll of beauty and tranquillity that attracted artists to paint the landscape of rising hills and wooded areas, while visitors would arrive to enjoy the locally grown strawberries in the tea gardens. Farming was an important feature of the landscape too. Small fields abounded like a patchwork quilt all around the vicinity. This rural, romantic setting contrasted with the Victorian town of Plymouth with its high-density housing and tall, smoking chimneys that was so close, yet separated by the Cattewater.

Part of Lower Hooe edges around Hooe Lake. Here in this area there were eighteenth-century cottages where the poor working-class folk lived. They earned their living as quarrymen or watermen, the latter unloading the ships' cargoes that anchored in the Cattewater. Small boats were built on the shoreline at Hooe. The local men had only a short walk to go for a drink of beer at The Royal Oak, which had been converted from a barn. The public house was reputed to be haunted; there were stories of a woman who could be heard sobbing in one of the bedrooms.

Hooe Lake was associated with timber. Ships would arrive at the Cattewater and the cargo of timber would be unloaded, then secured as rafts and towed to Hooe Lake. Here it would be left to season by the Oreston Timber yard. The floating wood was a playground for children in spite of the safety risks. They were able to get on to the timber rafts and walk across them, from one side of the lake to the other.

The Forts

Above West Hooe is Fort Stamford and beyond that the larger Fort Staddon. Both forts were built in 1867. Five years later heavy guns were placed at Stamford. The building of these defences required the construction of a military road from Pomphlett to Staddon Heights, which meant acquiring land. In order for the work to go ahead, a farmhouse at Hooe had to be demolished. Notice was given to the vicar to give up his parsonage home and school. Notice of intent to build a road was also served to other landowners including Lord Morley and Colonel Harris. These proposals caused a considerable reaction by the villagers of Hooe. Their protests must have had some bearing on the final decision as none of the buildings were destroyed by the Ministry of Defence.

Stamford Fort occupies the site of defences that were prepared in 1643 in preparation for the loyalist siege. The Royalists who occupied Plymstock set up a guard at West Hooe. A force of Parliamentarians that had sailed from Plymouth attacked the Royalists at West Hooe in which the manor-house, even though not destroyed, was badly damaged. The manor-house was never rebuilt, but instead at sometime a farmhouse was constructed on the site that survived well into the twentieth century. It was eventually demolished to make way for the construction of some small shops.

The Stamford soldiers favoured the Victoria Inn and they were known for ordering a jug of beer from which all of them would drink. Poor people of the village were known to arrive at the Army cook house, situated next to the fort, hoping they would be given some of the food that otherwise would have been thrown away. It was not uncommon when soldiers were to depart from the camp to go around the village offering some of their personal belongings to raise money, to settle their debts.

In the nineteenth and twentieth century the military presence at both forts had links with Hooe village. Hexton House, Hooe, was used as a bakery to supply bread for the troops, a service that continued until 1903. Then, a Mr Wakeham of Oreston used the premises as a butcher's shop until 1932 when it reverted back to a private house.

The Irish militia were stationed at Stamford Fort at the beginning of the twentieth century. They arrived at Oreston by boat then made their way up to the fort, much to the delight of the local girls! Some village girls married soldiers who were stationed at Stamford. On a Sunday the men, dressed in their smart blue uniforms and pillbox hats, marched down the hill to attend parade at St John's Church, Hooe.

The Church

Designed by a young architect from Truro, St John's Church, was opened in 1853 at a cost of £1,200, donated by public subscription. It had accommodation to take 250 worshippers and was shared by the villagers of Turnchapel.

St John's Church is constructed of stone in the English style. The original wooden turret had two bells but was replaced in 1893 by a stone structure that hung one bell. Part of the living was paid by the War Office and Admiralty. At this period fellowship was apparent when a villager died. It was a tradition of the small community to pay one's respects to a fellow villager. The coffin was carried by relays of bearers up the steep hill to the churchyard at Hooe. A large vicarage (St Anne's House) was built at Jennycliff, but was taken over by the Ministry of Defence in 1861 and used to accommodate Army officers. Thereafter, for the next 106 years, the vicarage was at the corner house at Turnchapel, opposite the road to Mount Batten.

Community and Industry

There was a time when there was a certain level of animosity between Hooe and Turnchapel, even though they were in close proximity to each other and shared certain services – for example, they both had the same village policeman. Mrs F. Wood (née Brewer), born in Lower Hooe, records an incident when Hooe's village maypole was stolen after it had been erected for the May Day celebrations. It was believed that the lads of Turnchapel were to blame, which resulted in the Turnchapel maypole being damaged. That said, the communities loved to let their hair down and a social highlight was the annual summer Carnival held at Hexton Path Road.

Hooe had two village pumps, one of them fixed in the wall at Higher Hooe, the other set in the wall opposite the Victoria Inn. The villagers could also take their buckets or jugs in which to collect water pure enough to drink from the chute at the head of Hooe Lake, the source of which being an underground stream that made its way from Staddon Heights.

The local children played in the village streets, the nearby beaches and in Ashery Wood. The street games tended to be seasonal, and children played with basic toys and equipment such as marbles, hoops and skipping ropes. They also chalked the pavement to play hopscotch.

The Westlake's farm herd grazed on Staddon Heights and supplied milk to the local people. The milk would be conveyed in a churn and transferred from a measured container into the customers' jug.

Lower Hooe, although never a large community, had at one time more buildings than West Hooe. Like the other villages in the immediate area it had links with quarrying. During the late-nineteenth century a small quarry at Hexton Hill had started working. As it was uneconomical to quarry the stone from where it was originally being taken, a tunnel, which took three years to complete, was cut by working from each end of the solid limestone quarry. The stone was then taken to the south shore of Hooe lake and shipped from the small quay. The quarry was abandoned in the early 1930s. This was the quarry that was used as an air-raid shelter during the Second World War.

To the north-east of Hooe Lake is the Radford Quarry, famous for its coloured limestone of red, greys and blue. The stone from Radford Quarry was used for many monuments and buildings, including the 'Marble Interior' of Brompton Oratory, at Kensington.

On Hexton Hill in the nineteenth century the houses were built close together. Washing would be strung up high on the clothes-lines between the buildings, giving it a nautical look. Over the years, the state of the property in this area deteriorated so much that it became something of a slum. Eventually the houses were demolished and replaced by modern dwellings. Hexton had a plantation and caves that were shrouded in mystery. Human skulls were discovered on the site during the early 1930s. People believed the caves led up to Radford House where there was a secret entrance, but no such place was ever found.

Upper Hooe never really had a community focal point. After the First World War, as houses were built along Hooe Road, there was a slow spread of property north of the road.

Radford House

A historic gem at Upper Hooe cum Plymstock that was demolished in the mid-1930s was Radford House, built in Radford Dip. This was not the original house associated with the great and the good of the Elizabethan age, as Radford House was rebuilt in the eighteenth century, the Elizabethan features being replaced with a Georgian style. Radford was an impressive mansion of some 50 rooms set in a valley amid parklands and gardens close to the head of Radford Lake. This was the home of the Harris family, and the original house is marked on sixteenth-century maps.

Christopher Harris was one of the most influential men during Queen Elizabeth I's reign and was knighted. He was a personal friend of Sir Francis Drake and to celebrate the defeat of the Spanish Armada, Harris organised a victory banquet at Radford in honour of the 'Captains' of the English Fleet. When Drake died, Christopher Harris acted as one of his executors. Harris was also a friend of Sir Walter Raleigh, but when Raleigh returned to England from his ill-fated expedition to Venezuela in search of the fabled land of El Dorado, he was arrested and held at Radford House for five weeks before travelling to London to go on trial. James I had him executed.

During the Civil War the area was a scene of fighting between the Royalists and the Parliamentarians and Radford House had been subjected to attack during the conflict.

In the eighteenth century a member of the Harris family married Catherine Bulteel of Flete House. From this union the Harris and Bulteel families were to reside at Radford House or in the small mansions on the estate grounds. In 1914 a member of the Bulteel family was imprisoned as the result of the financial collapse of The Royal Naval Bank. In 1917, a time when RNAS Cattewater was being built, the bankrupt Radford estate was put up for auction. The mansion with other properties and land went under the hammer and were purchased by a local man, Mr William Mitchell, who was to become the largest landowner in the area.

During the First World War Radford House was used to billet soldiers. There is a dearth of information about the house during the aftermath of the First World War other than Mitchell let the mansion out to various tenants. Lawrence of Arabia, when he was stationed at RAF Mount Batten, records visiting Radford House, and coming across what he believed was a Roman alter but although he faced scepticism as to nature of his find. Later in the archeological dig at Mount Batten, evidence revealed there had been a Roman presence in the area. What attracted Lawrence to Radford House ? It could have been its association with Walter Raleigh who, according to Lawrence, was a kinsman of the Chapman family on his father's side.

William Mitchell, the owner of Radford House, was involved in public life and highly respected. After he died of a sudden heart attack, the trustees considered restoring Radford House, but the costs of the repairs were prohibitive. In 1935 a decision was made for the mansion to be demolished. A gang of workers moved in who pulled down the building and they made a good job as not a single fragment of the house remained on the site. Other properties of the Radford estate that were sold off remain to this day. Relatives of Squire Bulteel (the Buteels were Huguenots) lived in the remaining larger houses of the estate. Hooe Manor (Bell Vue) was acquired by Colonel Coates. In later years the Colonel would supply foliage to decorate the gymnasium at RAF Mount Batten for the children's christmas party.

The Development of the Village

Until the late 1920s, Hooe tended to be something of an outback. There was at this time a concern about the danger of Hooe Road. Wing Commander Sydney Smith, the Commanding officer of the Batten flying boat station had written to the District Council expressing his fears because of the number of accidents along the winding route. Mr W. Mitchell supported Sydney Smith's concern. Mitchell had already offered his carriageway through Radford Park as a way of removing the dangers, by avoiding the steep Radford Hill. A plan was drawn up but the Rural District Council turned it down.

Times were changing for the villagers when in the late 1920s two private bus services started from Plymouth to Hooe. During 1931 electric street lighting was introduced in Hooe and within a year every street in the village was lit in this way and many families had the provision of electricity installed in their homes.

One event created some local excitement with the

first ever 'talkie' film shown in the village. About this time Mr Edwin Rogers was the headmaster of Hooe Church School. He was the father of the distinguished actor Paul Rogers. Other headmasters were Mr Standbury and Mr Rabley, who was in charge of the infant school at Hooe that was once housed in what is now the church hall. Each morning Mrs Stenning heated the children's milk in a bowl of hot water that stood on top of a stove. The stove was also used for heating this very large room. There were no private schools in Hooe or Turnchapel.

Hooe village down by the lake slowly expanded with more and more houses. All this activity and a growing population must have stimulated trade as Mr Tapper opened his shop, Lake Stores, soon after, and Hooe had a Post Office installed in Mrs Perry's shop in 1933.

The War at Hooe

Many of the older residents of Hooe have memories of the Second World War, with young men being called up to serve their country. The first to have his medical was Mr W. Larcombe. During the first winter of the war the bitterly cold weather resulted in Hooe Lake being frozen over. The air attacks on Plymouth meant that the Cattewater villages were always under threat of being bombed. From the end of June 1940 the air-raid warning frequently sounded. These nightly warnings, as well as the bombing, disturbed the sleep of the villagers. As early as 26 August 1940, at the time of the Battle of Britain, 13 high-explosive bombs were dropped in the vicinity of Hooe. Public and school air-raid shelters were built in Hooe, one of which was erected at Yonder Street. The Air Raid Precaution warden's post was a room at Hooe Social Club. The Hexton quarry shelter, referred to as 'the tunnel', was popular, as space was limited. The District Council issued permits to use the shelter.

The major fire that occurred at the nearby oil tanks at Turnchapel in 1940 had an impact on the community at Hooe. As the fire continued unabated a voluntary evacuation scheme was organised for people from Hooe to be accommodated at Plymstock and Goosewell School; later the villagers were evacuated to Plympton. Some 30 years later there was another serious fire in the area between Turnchapel and Hooe when petrol exploded close to six oil tanks. Another explosion ignited the oil tanks, resulting in local families being evacuated to Plymstock.

With the railway out of action and a reduced wartime bus service life became difficult for the villagers, although there was always the ferry service to visit Plymouth. On 21 March 1941 the second night of the Plymouth Blitz when the German Airforce continued to attack Plymouth, large numbers of incendiary bombs fell on Hooe and Turnchapel, together with high-explosive bombs. One bomb fell in a field behind West Hooe Farm causing damage to the farmhouse, another bomb demolished two council-houses.

One Hooe family's Home Front contribution to the war effort was to hand wash the shirts of servicemen, there were no washing machines then. Clothes-lines were hung high across the street with dozens of shirts pegged to the line blowing in the wind.

The People of Hooe

There are some famous people are associated with Hooe. One such is Helen Yate, the Olympic swimmer who competed in the London Olympics of 1948. Helen would travel up to London for her training as Plymouth did not have a swimming-pool of Olympic size. It is interesting to note that Sharon Davies lived at Plymstock for a time, so this rural area had as residents two of the most outstanding female swimmers this country has have ever produced.

June Whyte came to live at Hooe as a young school girl. Her grandfather was Henry Elford who owned the Red Funnel Ferry line and built property in the area. June was a founder member of the Hooe and Radford Preservation Society and served as its secretary for many years.

Hooe Today

The postwar years leading up to the new millennium gradually changed the face of Hooe, with the building of more council-houses and private property. In 1964 part of Hooe Lake was drained and grassed over and is now used as a recreation area. In later years crowds of people attended a meeting at Hooe to discuss the Hooe Lake Maritime project that proposed 400 berths should be provided for boat owners. Significant changes occurred when on 1 April 1967, Plymouth extended its boundaries to bring Hooe (and the other Cattewater villages) into its administration. Times changed when the historic Stamford Fort built in 1865 opened as a night club in July 1973. For the benefit of the villagers of Hooe and Turnchapel the community

hall opened on the 25 April 1981, near to the top of Church Hill. After 25 years it is still in use.

The Village of Turnchapel

The Cattewater villages originated as small independent communities. Although in close proximity, they are to a degree isolated from each other. Turnchapel's older properties are built along a steep narrow hill that continues down to the waterfront. The lie of the land dictates the shape of the old village and restricts its development, as it is built between a quarry face and the River Plym. The received view of the village depends on what has survived through time, as many of the older properties were demolished. We are thus left with few indicators as to the poverty or prosperity that once existed in the locality.

A residential area that is part of Turnchapel has been built on top of the local quarry. Turnchapel generated its own community life and social bonding. At one time the village was not always in accord with its nearby neighbours, as rivalry existed – a reason for which was the fierce competition for local jobs in hard times. There came a time, however, when the local communities of the villages began to mix. A tradition developed whereby a party of carol singers, made up of Turnchapel and Oreston men, would get together on Christmas Eve to spread good cheer around the parish, finishing up at the Castle Inn, Mount Batten. Other carol singers would also make their round, finishing up at the King's Arms, Oreston.

Throughout the years, as the villagers began to commute to work and outside forces brought to bear, the individuality of Turnchapel village and the social face of the community to some degree was lost.

Traditional Industry

Quarrying and shipbuilding have been major influences in the development of Turnchapel. There is reference to the area being used as a shipyard for the construction and fitting out of ships to fight the Spaniards, although surprisingly there is no mention of this in M. Oppenheim's *The Maritime History of Devon*. Heather Breeze in her interesting *History of Turnchapel* records the first residential building in the area was built by a sea captain in 1656, to be near his ship.

A 1768 map of Plymouth Sound does not mark Turnchapel, although this does not mean there was

Above: *This picture was taken by Plymouth photographer Stanley Green. The two Hooe children are standing with their gas-mask cases in the rubble of a building demolished by an enemy bomb, watching the smoke billowing up from the burning oil tanks at Turnchapel, in November 1940.*

Left: *One of the traumatic experiences for the Cattewater villages in the Second World War was when the Turnchapel oil tanks were set on fire by an enemy aircraft in November 1940. It was a concern that the plume of smoke that hovered above Plymouth would serve as a beacon for enemy aircraft to attack the city.*

Above: *One person who has lived in Hooe for many years is Helen Yate who represented Great Britain the London Olympics of 1948. Helen also represented England in the Empire Games in New Zealand. What is remarkable is that Helen, and Sharon Davies, arguably two of the finest women swimmers ever produced in the UK, lived so close together in this area.*

Above: *This delightful picture records the unveiling of the Hooe and Turnchapel Community Centre by the Deputy Lord Mayor of Plymouth, watched by Mrs Susan Trible, Derek England, Chief Constable John Anderson, and the local community constable Roy Wallace, 25 April 1981.*

An early 1950s view of Hooe, showing the swingbridge across Hooe Lake. The elongated building in the front is Hooe School. The picture clearly shows the geographic relationship with Turnchapel. On the left side of the lake is Barton Road that was widened by the American Army to allow their military forces to reach the Turnchapel Hards (Sycamore Beach) to load up their amphibious crafts for D Day.

no community there, as maps at this time were drawn for specific purposes. A 1779 map does indicate a small settlement, called Turn Chap. There is an unconfirmed story that the village obtained its name when troops on exercise there were ordered to 'turn at the chapel'. At the end of the seventeenth century Turnchapel was repairing Royal Navy ships, which included frigates. As ships being built were getting larger in size, dry docks were needed to examine them and undertake the necessary repairs. In 1793 the young Lord Boringdon ordered two slipways to be constructed at Turnchapel, along with a wet dock. This was located in an area of Turnchapel now used by the Royal Marines. The shipyard was leased to John Carter and then Isaac Blackburn, and hence became known as 'Blackburn's Dockyard'. The construction of this dock, started in 1800, became a challenge because of the problems encountered to make it watertight. It was finally completed in 1804, one year before the Battle of Trafalgar. The first Naval ship built in this dock, the *Derwent* took three years to complete. It was a 18-gun sloop rigged as a brig. Turnchapel at the time was the only privately owned shipbuilding yard in Devon. Among the other ships that

Blackburn built were two battleships, both of 74 guns: HMS *Armada* and HMS *Clarence*. The *Clarence* was launched on 11 April 1812 as crowds of people gathered from both sides of the Cattewater to witness the launch. An oil painting of the launch of HMS *Clarence* at Turnchapel can be seen at the Plymouth City Art Gallery.

In 1809 mooring chains were laid in the Cattewater that improved the commercial facilities of the place. The Turnchapel shipyard was sold to John Pope in about 1825, and the yard became known as 'Pope's Yard and Dry Dock'. One of Pope's orders was in 1832 when he built the first chain ferry for Saltash. Pope continued shipbuilding for well over 25 years but sold his interests, or what was left of them, in 1859. As Pope went bankrupt the yard was taken over by the Naval Bank. However, that too went bankrupt, which resulted in a number of people in the area loosing their savings.

Pope owned the Shipwright Arms, a Turnchapel public house built in 1790. Its name derived from the Turnchapel shipyard that according to Arthur Glinn, a one time resident of Turnchapel, was the largest yard outside Devonport. Whatever shipbuilding was taking place at Turnchapel there were few properties

A painting by John Rogers of the launch of HMS Clarence *at Turnchapel in 1812. It is thought that this was the biggest ship ever built in the Cattewater.*

in the village; a contemporary map shows there was simply a large orchard and garden close by.

If Oreston was well known for the number of captains who lived there, so Turnchapel was associated for its ships' pilots. Pilotage at the time was compulsory at Plymouth for vessels over 3,600 tons and for ships sailing outside home trade limits. There were two types of pilots. The Plymouth-licensed pilots at one time would cruise offshore, perhaps fishing, waiting for an arriving ship that would need a pilot to bring the ship to port. Then there were the harbour pilots, one time unlicensed pilots who would take over from the licensed pilots and bring the ship up to its berth. With the development of Plymouth in the mid-nineteenth century as a port of call for the ocean-going liners and merchant shipping there was a growing amount of work for pilots. The increase in traffic created a great deal of competition between pilots, especially those from Cawsand and Turnchapel. That said, even pilots from the same village would vie against each other. It was every man for himself, on sighting a ship they would race to be first on board to get the job. Large sailing cutters were later used. In addition to the crew they would sail with up to five pilots at the ready to board a ship.

Plymouth ships were recognised by the letter P and a number on their sail. In a 1830 directory 19 pilots are listed as being based in the Cattewater area. The 1891 census lists 12 pilots living at Turnchapel. The families of the pilots would be employed as crew on the pilot cutters. Phillip Cullis, John Pascho, Thomas Staddon, Charles Rodway are

names of some of the Turnchapel pilots. Prominent among the Turnchapel pilots were members of the Glinn family. In 1872 when Edward Glinn and his son were out rowing with three pilots the boat was run down by a liner that crushed the boat in two; all three pilots were drowned.

For so small a community Turnchapel had its local heroes. William Glinn, for example, was awarded a silver medal by the Dutch Government for rescuing the crew of a sinking dutch ship. The Plymouth area in 1899 experienced what was described as the worst storm for 30 years. The *Shamrock* in Mount Batten Bay was dragged by her anchor and ended up on the rocks. A tug was called out to help pull her off the rocks but it could not get near the ship. Some Turnchapel pilots and the crew of a cutter took their boarding boat to the Cattewater side of Mount Batten and, with the help of spectators, dragged the boat across the field and relaunched it on the seaward side. The pilots managed to keep their boat clear of the rocks to reach the ship and saved the five-man crew. They rowed back to the shore, 10 men in a 16-foot boat. The five Turnchapel pilots and the two man crew of the cutter received watches and medals from the Royal Humane Society. Two of the men were the sons of Andrew Glinn, who at one time was a Cawsand pilot but was sacked for smuggling. Four of Glinn's grandsons who lived at Turnchapel became pilots. Henry Glinn lived at Pinch's Cottage. The sailing cutters survived until the 1920s. One of the boats owned by a member of the Glinn family was sold and became a houseboat in Hooe Lake.

Turnchapel in the early part of the twentieth century, showing the New Inn. Here, in this lower part of the village, the poorer working-class people lived in tenanted property.

The Growth of a Community

As shipbuilding developed, men who came to work at Turnchapel brought their families and rented rooms. It gradually took on the semblance of a village with a community employed in the local shipyard, as watermen and maritime pilots. Later Trinity House became responsible for licensing pilots, producing a new generation of uniformed pilots, most of whom lived in Plymouth.

Lord Boringdon began building Boringdon Terrace, which was decorated with stucco and pedimented doorcases raised above the road. At one end of the terrace was the Boringdon Arms, while at the other was a property called the Manor House. The New Inn public house was built close to the village well, and replaced the small 1770 inn. Lord Boringdon was the freeholder of the Turnchapel shipyard and the elegant row of Georgian-style terraces. This suggests that Turnchapel was a closed village, that is, anything relating to the village, such as building work or selling local farm produce, could only be undertaken with permission from his lordship. In the mid-eighteenth century Turnchapel was a place without street lighting; not until 1928 were gas lamps

installed in the village. Properties at Turnchapel were once lit by oil-lamps that when carried from room to room cast long shadows, but these lamps produced a good source of light.

In the latter years of Queen Victoria's reign, Turnchapel men were mainly employed in the local shipyard, but with the opening of the Turnchapel ferry pier in 1889 men were attracted to seek work across the water in Plymouth. The ferry that had been working for 20 years now called at Oreston, Turnchapel, Mount Batten and Plymouth. In 1888 the London and South Western Railway had extended its line from nearby Plymstock to Turnchapel, but this was a more expensive way for the workmen to travel to the city centre. Many of the villagers were very poor; life was hard for these people. Turnchapel houses were often overcrowded as most of the premises were tenanted, some children sleeping six in a room. Children often went without basic provisions, such as shoes. There was no state pension for the elderly; if their family did not look after them, there was the possibility of receiving a pittance in charity. The alternative was to end up in the workhouse, a most depressing place in which to end one's life. Social change came about with the introduction of the Old Age Pension Act in 1908, which saw the

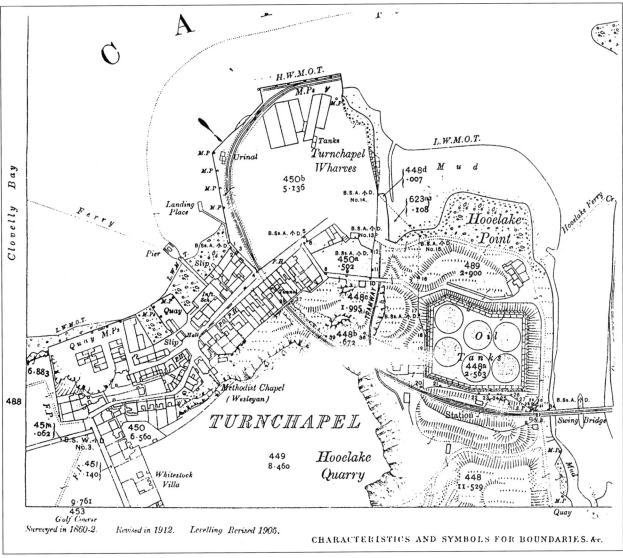

A map of Turnchapel published in 1904. The small village railway station was situated below the oil tanks and near the swingbridge, a distance away from the village sufficient to get one wet if it was raining. The map indicates the Hooe Lake ferry.

spectre of poverty for the aged lifted a small degree for many local poor people.

Those gainfully employed worked long hours for very low wages. One young Turnchapel girl was sent each Friday at midday to collect here father's wages from the dockyard. Having no money she would set out from Turnchapel and walk along the railway line into Plymouth, then on down Union Street to Devonport to meet her father at the dockyard gate where he handed his wages over to her. This ensured the wages were used for rent and food and not wasted on drink.

A Changing Village

Turnchapel had two schools, one a National mixed school for 124 children the other an infant school built in 1855 down on the Quay. The introduction of the 1870 Education Act meant school attendance was compulsory for all the village children. Despite this, poor parents of older children tended to defy the school attendance officer and send their children out to earn money.

The village whatever the plight of families at the turn of the century appeared to be self-sufficient, the village had five grocery shops and various residential tradesmen offering skilled services. Turnchapel's shipbuilding, however, was in decline; where there had been five shipbuilders living in Turnchapel in 1897 only one remained in 1900. The image of the village changed as industrial wharves were built in by the edge of the Cattewater together with the construction of large oil tanks for the Navy.

A postcard view of Turnchapel showing the ferry pier. The steep pathway amid the greenery led down to the disused iron-ore mine at Mount Batten.

High Days and Holidays

Turnchapel continued to see the young soldiers wander down from Fort Staddon to drink their ale in the local public houses. Much of the village social life was centred around the village church and chapel. Young girls wore pretty dresses made by their mothers when they went for their Sunday school outings and collected leaves and small flowers to press between the pages of their bible.

A special day in the year was May Day when the children dressed up and paraded in the 'lower town', where the May Queen and Boy King, together with their attendants, were chosen. Then off they would go in procession, led by a band up the hill to Well Field to be presented to the Colonel of the regiment. Each child was given an orange and a bag of sweets. Everyone sang the 'Song of May' before the children danced around the ribboned Maypole. On May Day visitors flocked to Mount Batten to spend their money on swings and the hoop-la stands.

Cheapjacks came from Plymouth selling their wares of streamers or windmills on sticks; it all added to the excitement.

During weekends and public holidays the streets of Turnchapel came alive with ferry passengers who travelled over from Phoenix Wharf, Plymouth, to make their way up to Staddon Heights or Bovisand. Territorial soldiers would arrive on Staddon Heights in the summer and camp in large white canvas bell tents. When the time came for them to depart the poor children of the villages would arrive to take away any army surplus food. In 1897 when Queen Victoria celebrated her reign of 'sixty glorious years' each village schoolchild was presented with a china mug showing the Queen's portrait and Union Jack. Turnchapel had a party to celebrate the occasion with dancing in the streets. The villagers then made their way to the top of Staddon Heights to watch and cheer as the soldiers formed a line a mile long and fired a *feu de joie*, a ceremonial salute of rapid-firing rifles.

Carnival on the Wellfield, Turnchapel. William Perry is in fancy dress as John Bull. The Carnival Queen is Bessie Dungey, to her left is the Maid of Honour, Hilda Pearse. The King was called Macdonald. This picture was taken before the Second World War.

Bell tents at Bovisand close to Mount Batten. It was a popular venue for visitors in the 1920s when this photograph was taken.

Eight girls and one young boy dressed as sailors, all members of Lily Symon's Dancing Class that participated in Turnchapel's 1938 Carnival. Left to right: Mavis Bond, Irene Burridge, Maureen Roberts, Una Glanville, Gloria Mears, Audrey Mears, Audrey Morgan, Doris Carpenter.

The 1920s and '30s

At the outbreak of the First World War the fear of invasion and bombardment from the German Navy led to sandbags and barbed wire entanglements being constructed along the coastline around Plymouth. The threat of an enemy attack increased the military presence up on Staddon Heights and additional troops were stationed at Bovisand Fort. Huge guns and searchlights were mounted at Jennycliff to cover the eastern entrance to Plymouth Sound, across which a boom defence had been installed to prevent the entry of enemy submarines.

In the aftermath of the First World War, Turnchapel remained a small, quiet village and although there was a little development and some properties changed hands, people tended to rent properties rather than buy them. Entertainment in the mid-1920s was very much a local affair and the vestiges of the Victorian way of life continued for some time. For example, indoors, families played parlour games, local amateur artistes from the nearby communities would provide a concert in the school next to the church and the magic lantern man would visit the village and show pictures of the wonders of the world or the antics of Felix the cat. As a special treat, people would perhaps visit Plymouth to enjoy a Christmas pantomime at the Palace theatre or go to one of the cinemas to watch a silent film starring Mary Pickford or Charlie Chaplin, although all this changed with the advent of movies with sound at the end of the 1920s. The church and chapel still provided an important focus for social life in the village, with organised socials and outings that meant a ride in a charabanc and a picnic tea. Those sports-minded young men of the village played for a local football team.

From 1922 until the 1970s Clovelly Bay was the permanent anchorage of the ships of the American

Upper Turnchapel taken from the Wellfield. Dartmoor is in the distance. Part of the field was RAF property. To the left of the picture can be seen the Mount Batten Guard House with the barrier up. The large double-fronted house down the bottom of the hill was for many years the Vicarage.

A recent picture of the restored Victorian rocket house above Turnchapel that had a gallant history of saving lives. The Mount Batten team of life-savers were volunteers from Hooe and Turnchapel.

This fine corner house at St John's Road was for many years the Vicarage. The property was sold in 1968 and a new Vicarage built behind St John's Church. A fine view of the golf course could be had from the front of the old Vicarage.

TURNCHAPEL V.E.DAY CELEBRATIONS - 8th MAY 1995
PROGRAMME OF EVENTS

All Day Vintage buses will run to and from City Centre from 11.00 am. refreshments and beers at Fort Stamford forecourt and the Marquee in the Village Car park, Ice Creams at Dale's Parlour, authentic music from private houses, Pubs open all day including tea, coffee, beers, snacks and meals, exhibitions of posters, photos, press cuttings, memorabilia etc in the New Inn, Fort Stamford and Boringdon Arms.

Morning Military and Vintage Vehicles Rally at Jennycliff car park. Sail past by yachts accompanying Royal Marine Landing Craft with Jazz Band "The Cats Whisker" playing

Noon Band lands at Turnchapel and proceeds to Fort Stamford

12.30 Trips on Landing Craft out to the Sound from R.M. Slipway Fireworks from Fort Stamford Ramparts

12.40 Military and vintage vehicles parade into Fort Stamford car park

13.00 Fort Stamford: Beer at 6d per half pint (1945 coins, no change!) as long as the firkin lasts

13.30 Vehicles parade through Village

14.00 Jazz Band "Riverside Sound" plays in Village Centre Punch and Judy Show, Boringdon Terrace

14.30 New Inn: Beer at 6d per ½ pint (1945 coins) while it lasts

15.00 Radio Broadcast of Peace announcement

15.30 Plymouth Maids dance from Garden to Marquee Village Children's Tea Party on Boringdon Terrace

16.00 Live Music and Radio Broadcasts in Marquee Marquee: Beer at 6d per ½ pint (1945 coins) while it lasts

17.30 Last trips on Landing Craft

18.00 Firework Finale near Marquee

20.00 Streets open to traffic

20.30 Meet at Mount Batten Tower for National Two Minute Silence

20.40 H.M.S. Argyle fires salute, Lighting of Beacon and fireworks immediately after Two Minute Silence Bar-be-que near Tower, view of Hoe: fireworks, lasers there later.

21.00 Live music in New Inn and Boringdon Arms

Midnight Bars Close

Above: The 50th VE Day celebrations were a happy occasion for the residents of Turnchapel. There was a full programme of events that concluded with a beacon being lit at Mount Batten, by Mrs Dale Philip, of Turnchapel.

Right: The 1949 Carnival Queen of Turnchapel. Vera Becker is crowned Queen by Revd L. Pike, with Jean Carpenter (left) and Sylvia Hurrell (right) as her Maids of Honour.

As part of the VE Day 50th anniversary celebrations Mrs Dale Philip used her house as an ice-cream parlour. As it was a fine day all the village celebrations were held outside, except for the two Turnchapel public houses that were packed throughout the day.

Cable Company. One advantage associated with the ships' presence was that they gave employment to men from the local villages. For many years the local steam ferry would call on the ships each day to drop or collect workers. These ships were used to lay cable under the sea, perhaps across the Atlantic. The local men were often away from home for long periods of time.

Up to 1928, before the introduction of bus services from Plymouth, people crossing over Laira Bridge would soon notice the abrupt change from urban Plymouth to a rural environment. Turnchapel in the 1930s retained a few general shops and a limited postal service. The villagers were mainly working-class and the poorer families tended to live in the lower part of the village, while the middle-class residents lived in the substantial houses along St John's Road. The national economy at the time was a cause for concern and there were few local jobs to be had. Turnchapel men would stand around week after week near Elford's ferry pier; suddenly there would be a rush down to the water and some half-dozen boats or more would set out as fast as the men could row towards Plymouth Sound as news came in that a

ship laden with timber was arriving. Hopes would rise that some of the men would be taken on as temporary stevedores, assisting in unloading the ship. At the most only two or three would be given a job from up to 30 men.

Harold Pascho, a member of a well known Turnchapel family was rather more fortunate as he had a job as an insurance clerk in an office in central Plymouth near to what was then Spooner's Corner. Like many other villagers he would take the ferry to Phoenix Wharf pier and walk the rest of the way to work. Harold recalls going to play tennis in one of the Mount Batten hangars, the court being roughly marked out. He was allowed to do this as his brother-in-law was stationed at the flying boat base.

If Oreston had a successful football team, Mrs Alice Greet of Turnchapel was in advance of her time as she at the age of 67 formed the Turnchapel Ladies Football Club in the late 1930s. It won its first match beating Hooe.

The Second World War

The war was always at the doors of the local villages. During the Plymouth Blitz of 1941 there was a great exodus of people each evening from the city, an official figure of 50, 000 is recorded. The trekkers took to the the countryside outside the city centre to seek a safe haven and if they could, get a night's rest. These nocturnal refugees travelled out of Plymouth in all directions; some arrived at Turnchapel or Oreston and made their way up the narrow lane to Jennycliff or Staddon Heights. The trekkers would settle down, but there was always the risk they would be moved on by the police as much of the land was in the hands of the defence authorities. On occasions, it would have been very noisy as there was an anti-aircraft gun battery on Staddon Heights. It was a disturbing experience for these people to look across the waters of the Sound and see their city, possibly their own homes, being destroyed by the German Airforce. Other trekkers who arrived at Oreston by ferry would make their way to the school Plymstock at where a rest centre had been established.

During the Second World War the Mackay-Bennett cable ship, known as the 'haunted ship' after picking up bodies from the infamous 1912 *Titanic* disaster, was sunk by enemy aircraft in 1941 at the time RAF Mount Batten was attacked. For 15 months it lay submerged in Clovelly Bay with its masts showing above the water. The developing technology of radio

A postcard picture of Oreston's waterfront, taken early in the twentieth century, showing a steam ferry arriving at the landing stage. Not a busy scene, but there are a number of men standing outside the King's Arms.

A public notice regarding the introduction of a ferry service from Oreston to Plymouth encouraging Plymouthians to visit the beautiful countryside in the vicinity of Radford, Hooe and Staddon Heights, 3 May 1869.

telecommunications resulted in a reduction in the use of cable and the 'Turnchapel ships' were taken away from their moorings. Now in the twenty-first century there is a complete contrast in Clovelly Bay as a multitude of marine craft are anchored in the marina.

Preparing for D Day, a concrete 'chocolate-box hard' was laid down at Sycamore Beach, Turnchapel, where amphibious craft were loaded with troops and equipment ready for the invasion of Europe. Barton Road adjacent to Hooe Lake had been widened and reinforced by an American Army construction company to allow the movement of tanks and other heavy transport to load at the hard.

Out with her mother in Hooe Road, Mary Outhwaite of Turnchapel recalls waving to the American soldiers who would throw sweets and cigarettes to the locals as they passed by in military convoys. The Americans would have arrived from high-security assembly camps on the fringe of

Dartmoor and followed a route through Plymstock. Closer to the River Plym the Saltram estate was a place where large numbers of Americans also assembled with their military vehicles. Here in the wooded areas of Saltram men carved their names or initials and a date on the bark of the trees as a record of their presence. It is possible these American servicemen embarked at Sycamore Beach.

The residents of Turnchapel, along with the rest of the nation, suffered years of austerity when the war was finally over. The village celebrations that took place to mark the 60th anniversary of VE-Day on 8 May 1995 will be remembered as one of the days the spirit of Turnchapel prevailed. The villagers organised a whole day of events. The flags were put out; red, white and blue bunting was everywhere. The publicity generated for the event brought people in buses from Plymouth. Near the end of the day everyone made for Mount Batten to meet by the ancient round tower, where a two-minute silence was observed. Thereafter a beacon was lit, followed by a fireworks display. The revelry continued as people danced in the streets of Turnchapel until midnight.

The Village of Oreston

Close to Oreston is Plymstock, once one of the gateways to Plympton, a place at one time more important than Plymouth. The two said villages were once separated by rural countryside, but now a main road separates them. Oreston is the oldest of the Cattewater villages and at one time known as Osum, whereas a map of 1779 names the village Oston. In 1868 a hoard of early Bronze Age implements was discovered a mile from Oreston under a flat stone a couple of feet below the surface.

Elias Warley of Oreston, one of the village men that became a merchant seaman. He contracted typhoid fever and died at the age of 25. Warley was the grandfather of the local historian, the late Dorothy Warley Pitt.

Ernest Tope was one of the captains of Oreston. He, like many mariners of the time, went to sea without a wireless. He was taken ill at sea and died in the Channel Islands in February 1919, leaving a widow and two sons.

The location of Oreston was important, as it was once the home of the ferry terminal on the direct route from Cattedown to Plymstock. This ancient ferry that was known to be working in the mid-fifteenth century continued its service up to the period of the 1920s.

References to the presence of the Navy in the Cattewater are mentioned elsewhere in this book, but there is only fragmentary records as to Oreston's involvement. What is known is that during the early-eighteenth century Oreston was a place for a Naval gunpowder magazine. Oreston at the time was a fishing village with a harbour and quay linked to the fishing trade of Newfoundland. The harbour was reclaimed in the 1960s when the waterfront was extended.

The construction of the Plymouth Breakwater brought employment to Oreston, as the local quarry supplied thousands of tons of stone. The work started in 1812 and took over 30 years of demanding physical toil to complete. The quarried stone was taken out to the Plymouth Sound in specially built barges. At the quarry unsuitable stone was not discarded but kept and used for the beds and basins that were being constructed at Devonport Dockyard. The exploitation of quarried limestone also came into play in the expanding agriculture market, as burnt lime had beneficial results when treating acid soils. In the Cattewater area the quarries had their own limestone kilns, while limestone was also shipped out to kilns along the Tamar valley and nearby coastal communities.

There was once an oysterage in the Cattewater where the oysters were dredged. From the eighteenth until the early-twentieth century it was a traditional privilege that Oreston folk could go down onto the shore and gather the shells. This came to an end when the customary right to take oysters was threatened by someone who had leased a large cottage on the waterfront and prevented the villagers from taking the oysters. The villagers reacted and appealed to the law, which resulted in the order being rescinded.

If Turnchapel was known for its pilots, Oreston was the place where the captains of ships and barges lived and retired to; many of these resident mariners erected a flagstaff in their gardens. Most of the vessels of which the captains were in charge were sailing ships whose presence could be seen in and around the waters of Plymouth up to the period of the First World War. In the 1880s, Oreston was a place where little ships created a glorious sight when they were anchored in the Cattewater. Most of the vessels were Oreston ketches. There were also schooners from the western ports of Padstow and Bideford, with rivermen from Chester, Gloucester and Faversham. The 'mud' was a splendid anchorage in which to shelter from the storms; it was not uncommon for up to 70 ships to be seen riding out the gales in this spot.

A picture of Oreston in the early part of the twentieth century. The village bakery is on the left.

Some Captains of Oreston

Stephen Carter		*Bessie Simmons*
H. Davies	Schooner	*Thomas Edwin*
	Ketch	*John Rees*
J. Ellis	Ketch	*Plover*
Phillip Ellis	Smack	*The Providence*
Charles Holten	Schooner	*The Elinor*
J. Holten	Ketch	*Susan*
Jack Johns		*Lewisham*
William Palmer	Smack	*Yealm**
Bill Tope	Schooner	*Flower of Port Sole*
J. Tope	Ketch	*Advance*
John Tope	Ketch	*Fanny*
George Warley	Ketch	*The Fruiter*
George Wyath	Schooner	*Gertrude*
George Passmore	Sloop	*Edwin***

Apparently the Cattewater sailor was not enamoured with shipyards and when an Oreston owner bought a schooner he would often alter it into a ketch. This would require less labour and he could sail her with one less hand on board. The many captains of Oreston of the 1880s included such names as Philip Ellis with *Little Jane*, Harry Holberton – *Thomas*, Joseph Holten – *Plover*, Alfred Kingwell – *Lurine*, William Holten – *William W. Pearce*, Albert Trope – *Thomas Edwin*, Charlie Barker – *John Rees*, Harry Ellis – *Alfred Rooker*, George Tope – *Little Ruth*, Edward Willis – *Richard and Jane*. It was not unusual in the 1880s for men to arrive at Oreston in an Oreston-owned ship, which they had joined at another port, and marry an Oreston maid. Will Crooks's father came to Oreston from Hartlepool in Captain Stephen Carder's schooner and married the captain's daughter. Many captains continued to live in Oreston up to the time of the Second World War. An Oreston captain may not have his own vessel, but if he did and it was mortgaged, this was not necessarily a reflection of financial instability. The usual pattern for the running of the vessel was to divide the takings into three parts. The captain and his mate each received one third of the amount earned. The remaining share went to the vessel. The master was often a shareholder and sometimes the managing owner. Although the captains of Oreston were not really an elite, the local villagers tended to look upon them as a special group. There were parties held at the King's Arms public house in Oreston which only the captains and their families attended.

The *Yealm** was a smack of just under 33 tons built in 1878 by David Banks of Queens Ann's Battery, Plymouth, which traded up and down the River Tamar. Later William Palmer purchased her and used her as a coasting barge. After 50 years' service the *Yealm* ended up at Kingswear on the River Dart.

The *Edwin*** was a sloop that carried a top sail built in 1880 by the Oreston/Cattedown shipbuilder Richard Hill. The *Edwin* was engaged in the limestone trade mainly within the bounds of Plymouth, but sometimes there would be a run to Falmouth or Salcombe. Her master and mate William Maynes were both from Oreston.

The romance of Oreston is enhanced by its link to Alexander Selkirk, frequently cited as Daniel Defoe's inspiration for *Robinson Crusoe*. Selkirk, a seaman from Largo had been marooned on Juan Fernandez Island in the Pacific Ocean for five years before he was rescued in 1711. He did not spend long on land, however, and eight months after his return he was back at sea. He joined the Navy in 1717, becoming a Petty Officer on HMS *Weymouth*. While the ship docked at Plymouth in 1720 Selkirk became friendly with a woman some 20 years his senior, Frances Candish (sometimes given as Candes), who ran one of the village public houses. The couple wed before Selkirk set sail again at the end of 1720. Selkirk died at sea the following year.

The Growth of Methodism

Members of a Non-established Church were not allowed to be buried in the village graveyard at Oreston and were interred in the Dissenters' cemetery

Above: *The passage of time has altered the old quayside at Oreston, but this is how it looked in 1903. The man rowing the boat, Mr H. Pile, was the landlord of the King's Arms. The redevelopment of Oreston's waterfront took place in 1958 when many of the old buildings were demolished and significant alterations made to the quay.*

Right: *Situated near Plymouth and RAF Mount Batten there was always a risk that bombs would fall on the small community and many of the villagers lost their lives. In spite of their adversity people came smiling through, as shown by these householders at Thorneville Villas, 30 April 1944.*

Carnival time in Oreston in the late 1930s, with the Norsworthys and Colemans together with Mrs Ellis.

A wartime picture of Oreston men who were employed on the local steam ferry, 1917. They include Captain Philip Ellis, the man with the beard. Andy Tucker is standing at the back with his arms crossed and his cousin Bill Tucker is in front, holding the hand rail.

Plymstock Lane, Oreston. This was the old travellers' way when they made their way across the Cattewater from Cattedown by ferry to Oreston, then on to Plymstock.

at Pomphlett. This changed with the growth of the Methodist Church in Oreston due to the increase in the number of worshippers. In 1789, when Charles Wesley visited nearby Plymouth, the Oreston Methodists totalled 14 members; by 1816 the congregation had increased to 74. This must have influenced the elders to build a new church, constructed on land and using £250 contributed by the Duke of Bedford. The church stone was laid by Mr Mildmay, the local Member of Parliament, who was later knighted and became master of Flete House. The disused Methodist church became Chievely Hall and was used by the local community as the village hall.

Religion and drinking flourished side by side for a while at Oreston. At one time there were five public houses in Oreston but as time went on, maybe because of a change in the local economy, or perhaps

as a result of the growing influence of Methodism, only one public house survived. This public house, once managed by Frances Candish, who had married Alexander Selkirk, was purchased by a Methodist, who then closed it down.

The size of the village population during the nineteenth century can be judged when the vicar of Plymstock petitioned for a license to be issued for the Church of the Good Shepherd; a figure of 1,200 people was submitted as the number of people living within one mile of the church.

Work and Play

Oreston had its boat builders. During the eighteenth century William Lambell was a prominent figure of the village who leased three cottages. In the grounds of one of them he constructed a small shipbuilding

The homecoming of Sergeant F. Tucker of Oreston, his wife and son walking by his side. Crowds turned out to welcome him home, Union Jacks were flown. This is a famous Second World War picture used in many books.

yard where the sailing ship HMS *Hamoaze* was built. Mr Piles, another Oreston shipbuilder, was based in two old limestone buildings that stood on the waterfront for his shipbuilding activities. Piles was known to be the victualler of the King's Arms public house.

The increase in shipping arriving in the Cattewater created employment for men as stevedores. This was, however, a competitive way of earning a living and was rather poorly paid.

Oreston was where Henry Elford lived. He was a one-time farmer, who became the owner of the local steam ferry company.

By the end of the nineteenth century, men worked at the quarry at Oreston, extracting stone that was needed for the construction of buildings in Plymouth; the Naval town was rapidly growing in size.

There was also employment at the Oreston timber yard. Robert Bayly, owner of the yard, at one time employed 70 men. Very much a benevolent man he donated land for the construction of the reservoir dam at Burrator on Dartmoor, providing the stone from his Langshill quarry at Oreston. Bayly also gave the top of the quarry to the villagers of Oreston for use as a site for public recreation. The Old Library Cottage in Park Lane, Oreston, was once a library for use by Bayly's employees where they could come and borrow books for a halfpence per week.

Folklore has it that Oreston ladies were more attractive than those from the other nearby villages; they once had a reputation for dressing well, according to their social station. It was said that an Oreston lady could be recognised out in the street by the way she dressed. As far as the Oreston men were concerned they became famous for their breakwater crew that rowed a large cutter in the races of the local regattas.

The community spirit of Oreston was strong during the times between the wars: football had been a cornerstone of village activity and there were keen supporters in those days who would set out in motor carriages to support Oreston Rovers. In their time

they had been a very successful team. For the older village folk there was the Oreston and District bowling club.

The Impact of the War Years

The First World War brought many changes to Oreston. Not only did the young men go away to fight, but the quarrying of stone was drastically reduced. During the aftermath of the war more houses were built, increasing the village population, as people were migrating to houses being built in rural areas outside Plymouth; they wanted to live away from the densely packed residential areas of the Naval town and sought a better environment in which to live. Full-time employment in the village was a problem, but with the available local transport, except a bus service, men sought work in Plymouth.

The Second World War brought tragedy to Oreston when several people lost their lives through bombing. For example, Mrs Doris Newbury and her young daughter were killed on the 23 April 1941 when three high-explosive bombs demolished their home at Park Crescent. Some 2,000 incendiary bombs fell on Oreston during April 1941 at the time of the Plymouth Blitz. This brief reference does not reflect the number of other bombs and damage that the Cattewater villages, including the nearby communities of Elburton, Pomphlett and Plymstock.

Oreston Today

Throughout the latter decades of the twentieth century there have been further changes in Oreston. Many of the old limestone buildings of the village have been demolished, the old quayside is now gone, having been filled in as part of the redevelopment of the waterfront. Modern houses now sit alongside the properties of the old village, reflecting the fact the village has continued to evolve.

Bibliography

Anthony, Mary, *The Red Funnel Line*, private publication, 1990.

Avery, John, G., *The Cable Ships of Turnchapel*, Beech Books, 2004 .

Baff, K.C, *Maritime is No 10. A History of No. 10 Squadron RAAF*, private publication, 1983 .

Beadell, Dennis, *The Grangers of Turnchapel*, private publication.

Lord Blythe, Robin, *The History of Hooe Barton Farm*, The Friends of Hooe Barn, 2001.

Breeze, Helen, *The History of Turnchapel*, Radford and Hooe Lake Preservation Association, 2001.

Buttler, Tony, *Short Sunderland,* Warpaint series no 25, Hall Park Books.

Carter, Ian, *Coastal Command*, Ian Allen, 2004.

Clamp, Arthur, *Hooe and Turnchapel Remembered*, private publication, 1981.

Clamp, Arthur, *Oreston and its People Remembered*, private publication.

Clamp, Arthur, *Plymstock in Perspective*, private publication, 1992.

Cuncliffe, Barry, *Mount Batten Plymouth: A prehistoric and Roman Port*, Oxford University Committee for Archaeology, 1988.

Duffy, Michael, et al, *The New Maritime History of Devon Vol. 1*, Conway Maritime Press, 1992.

Gardiner, Julie, *Resurgan! Archaeology at Stonehouse, Mount Batten and Mount Wise Regeneration Areas, Plymouth*, Plymouth Museum, 2000.

Georgina ?, *Georgina recalls her early days in Turnchapel*, ND, Private publication.

Gill, Crispin, *Plymouth River. A history of the Laira and Cattewater*, Devon Books, 1997.

Information of Ministry, *Merchant Airmen*, HMSO, 1946.

Kingdom, Anthony, *The Turnchapel Branch*, Oxford Publishing Co., 1982.

Langdon, Ivy, *The Plymstock Connection*, West Country Books, 1995.

Osman, W.H., *Pigeons in World War Two*, The Racing Pigeon Publishing Co., 1950.

Pilborough, G., *History of RAF Marine Craft*, Canimpex.

Pitt Warley, Dorothy, *Recollections of the Plymstock Area*, private publication.

Pye, Andrew and Woodward, Freddy, *The Historic Defences of Plymouth*, Cornwall County Council, 1996.

Redman, Edgar, *The Air Force Reserve Depot, Radford*, paper read at Plymstock Civic Society, April 1940.

Rusbridger, James, *Who Sank the 'Surcouf'*, Ebury Press, 1991.

Smith, Graham, *Devon and Cornwall Airfields in the Second World War*, Countryside Books, 2000.

Smith Sydney, Clare, *The Golden Reign*, Cassell, 1940.

Stansky, Peter, *Sassoon. The worlds of Philip and Sybil*, Yale University Press, 2003.

Steele, Brian, *A history of Radford*, Radford Centre, 1990.

Stetzler, Marjorie F., *London Gazette* Devon Extracts, *Plymouth 1665–1765*, Devon Family History Society, 1989.

Stuart, Elisabeth, *Lost Landscapes of Plymouth*, Sutton Publishing, 1991.

Sturtivant, R. and Page, G., *Royal Navy Aircraft Serials and Units 1911–1919*, Air Britain (Historians) Ltd, 1992.

Sutherlans, Jon and Canwell, D., *The RAF Rescue Service 1918–1986*, Pen and Sword, 2005.

Tapley, W.G., 'Dissertation on the Radford Ward', c.1970.

Teague, Dennis, *Strike First. 'They shall not pass unseen'*, Baron Jay, 1982.

Teague, Dennis and Peter, White, *A Guide to the Airfields of South Western England*, Baron Jay, 1982.

Teague, Dennis, *Mount Batten: Flying Boat Base, Plymouth, 1913–1986*, Westway Publications, 1986.

Whyte, June, *Acquisition and Early Days of Mount Batten from Naval and Military Records*, Radford & Hooe Lake Preservation Association, 1995.

Wood, F.E., 'Recollections of Hooe', not published, 1977.

Websites used

www.plymouth.gov.uk
www.nationalarchives.gov.uk
www.fleetairarm.com
www.rafmuseum.org.uk
www.iwmcollections.org.uk
www.telawrence.inf/general/intro

Subscribers

Irene H. Ainsworth, Hooe, Devon
Tom Alcock, Hooe, Plymouth
A.E. Allsop, Plymstock, Devon
Mary Anthony, SHQ Mount Batten
Dave Ashbee, RAF Mount Batten 1963–1986
Ken Badge, Turnchapel
Nigel and Pam Baring, Hooe
David Andrew Bennett, University of Paisley, Ayr Campus, Scotland
Mr Richard John Bird
Mr David G. Brown, Oreston, Devon
Mr E. Burridge, Hooe
John, son of Sam, Burridge, Plymouth, Devon
K.J. Burrow, Bucks Cross, Devon
Edward Cartner, Penultimate Commanding Officer
Sheila Coleman, Hooe, Devon
Joyce Collins and Edith Joyce Dixon, Turnchapel
Sylvia Cooke, Hooe, Devon
Dennis and Doris Dean, Hooe, Plymouth
Mollie Dean (née Hine), Turnchapel and Hooe
Stuart R. Dolton, Hooe
Janet and David Dungworth, Mount Batten, Plymouth
Roy Eddison, Princess Crescent
June and Derek England, Hooe, Devon
Elizabeth A. Evans, Plymstock, Devon
Christopher Goodwyn, Mutley, Plymouth
John and Fiona Hamilton, St Annes House, Hooe, Plymouth
Sqn Ldr J.E.G. Hancock DFC, Plymouth
Sylvia Hiscock (née Pile), Plymouth
Adrian and Bev Holmes, Turnchapel, Plymouth
Mrs M.H. (Peggy) Hugo, Plymouth
Alan Izon, Solihull
Mr T. Darell Jago, Plymouth, Devon
Flt/Sgt Paddy Jamison
Joan and David King, Staddiscombe, Plymouth
Wg Cdr A.W.L. Mahon, Wimborne
Dr Linda McKeer, Plymstock, Devon
P.S. McMillan, Exmouth, Devonshire
Keith H. McMinn, Plymstock, Devon

Neill P.G. Mitchell
Keith Moorhouse, Plymstock, Devon
Ex CH/TECH Frank Morris, ASR/MCS SW
David J. Morris, Mount Batten, Devon
David and Jean Naylor, Plymstock, Devon
B.J. Northey, Mount Batten
Mary S. Outhwaite, Turnchapel
Dennis J. Peach, Ex Chief/TECH ASR/MCS
G.J. Pearse and Family
Norma Perry (née Pearse), Turnchapel
Roger Philp, Plymstock, Devon
Miss A.J. Prizeman, Plymouth
Sylvia L. Ridgway (née Perry), Turnchapel
Mr A.C. Roberts, Oreston, Devon
Colin Shepheard, Fleet Engineer, Mount Batten
Pieter Shipster, Shefford, Bedfordshire
Shirley and Rodney Smith, Plymstock, Devon
Barry and Sandra Stephens (Scouse), RAF Mount Batten, Plymouth
Joan G. Taskis, Plymouth, Devon
Raymond G.D. Thomas, Turnchapel
Kathleen Thomas, Turnchapel, Devon
Mr D.R. Thompson, Plymstock, Devon
Graham Thorne, Maldon
Gregory Stephen Unwin, Plymstock
John F.W. Walling, Newton Abbot, Devon
Eamonn Walsh
Mervyn George Warley (in memory of)
Mrs June Wheeler, Sunnyside, Turnchapel, Devon
H.B. Winstanley, Plymstock

Community Histories:
Further Reading

The Book of Addiscombe • Canning and Clyde Road
Residents Association and Friends
The Book of Addiscombe, Vol. II • Canning and Clyde Road
Residents Association and Friends
The Book of Ashburton • Stuart Hands and Pete Webb
The Book of Axminster with Kilmington • Les Berry
and Gerald Gosling
* The Book of Axmouth & the Undercliff •
Ted Gosling and Mike Clement
The Book of Bakewell • Trevor Brighton
The Book of Bampton • Caroline Seward
The Book of Barnstaple • Avril Stone
The Book of Barnstaple, Vol. II • Avril Stone
The Book of The Bedwyns • Bedwyn History Society
* The Book of Bere Regis • Rodney Legg and John Pitfield
The Book of Bergh Apton • Geoffrey I. Kelly
The Book of Bickington • Stuart Hands
The Book of Bideford • Peter Christie and Alison Grant
Blandford Forum: A Millennium Portrait • Blandford Forum
Town Council
* The Book of Blofield • Barbara Pilch
The Book of Boscastle • Rod and Anne Knight
The Book of Bourton-on-the-Hill, Batsford and Sezincote •
Allen Firth
The Book of Bramford • Bramford Local History Group
The Book of Breage & Germoe • Stephen Polglase
The Book of Bridestowe • D. Richard Cann
* The Book of Bridgwater • Roger Evans
The Book of Bridport • Rodney Legg
The Book of Brixham • Frank Pearce
The Book of Buckfastleigh • Sandra Coleman
The Book of Buckland Monachorum & Yelverton •
Pauline Hamilton-Leggett
The Book of Budleigh Salterton • D. Richard Cann
The Book of Carharrack • Carharrack Old
Cornwall Society
The Book of Carshalton • Stella Wilks and Gordon
Rookledge
The Parish Book of Cerne Abbas • Vivian and
Patricia Vale
The Book of Chagford • Iain Rice
The Book of Chapel-en-le-Frith • Mike Smith
The Book of Chittlehamholt with
Warkleigh & Satterleigh • Richard Lethbridge
The Book of Chittlehampton • Various
The Book of Codford • Romy Wyeth
The Book of Colney Heath • Bryan Lilley
The Book of Constantine • Moore and Trethowan
The Book of Cornwood and Lutton • Compiled by
the People of the Parish
The Book of Crediton • John Heal

The Book of Creech St Michael • June Small
The Book of Crowcombe, Bicknoller and Sampford Brett •
Maurice and Joyce Chidgey
The Book of Crudwell • Tony Pain
The Book of Cullompton • Compiled by the People
of the Parish
The Book of Dawlish • Frank Pearce
The Book of Dulverton, Brushford,
Bury & Exebridge • Dulverton and District Civic Society
The Book of Dunster • Hilary Binding
The Book of Easton • Easton Village History Project
The Book of Edale • Gordon Miller
The Ellacombe Book • Sydney R. Langmead
* The Book of Elmsett • Elmsett Local History Group
The Book of Exmouth • W.H. Pascoe
* The Book of Fareham • Lesley Burton and
Brian Musselwhite
The Book of Grampound with Creed • Bane and Oliver
The Book of Gosport • Lesley Burton and
Brian Musselwhite
The Book of Haughley • Howard Stephens
The Book of Hayle • Harry Pascoe
The Book of Hayling Island & Langstone • Peter Rogers
The Book of Helston • Jenkin with Carter
The Book of Hemyock • Clist and Dracott
The Book of Herne Hill • Patricia Jenkyns
The Book of Hethersett • Hethersett Society
Research Group
The Book of High Bickington • Avril Stone
The Book of Honiton • Gerald Gosling
The Book of Ilsington • Dick Wills
* The Book of Kessingland • Maureen and Eric Long
The Book of Kingskerswell • Carsewella Local
History Group
The Book of Lamerton • Ann Cole and Friends
Lanner, A Cornish Mining Parish • Sharron
Schwartz and Roger Parker
The Book of Leigh & Bransford • Malcolm Scott
The Second Book of Leigh & Bransford • Malcolm Scott
The Book of Litcham with Lexham & Mileham • Litcham
Historical and Amenity Society
The Book of Loddiswell • Loddiswell Parish
History Group
The New Book of Lostwithiel • Barbara Fraser
The Book of Lulworth • Rodney Legg
The Book of Lustleigh • Joe Crowdy
The Book of Lydford • Compiled by Barbara Weeks
The Book of Lyme Regis • Rodney Legg
The Book of Manaton • Compiled by the People
of the Parish
The Book of Markyate • Markyate Local History Society
The Book of Mawnan • Mawnan Local History Group
The Book of Meavy • Pauline Hemery
The Book of Mere • Dr David Longbourne
The Book of Minehead with Alcombe • Binding and Stevens

The Book of Monks Orchard and Eden Park • Ian Muir
and Pat Manning
The Book of Morchard Bishop • Jeff Kingaby
* *Mount Batten – The Flying Boats of Plymouth* •
Gerald Wasley
* *The Book of Mulbarton* • Jill and David Wright
The Book of Mylor • Mylor Local History Group
The Book of Narborough • Narborough Local
History Society
The Book of Newdigate • John Callcut
The Book of Newtown • Keir Foss
The Book of Nidderdale • Nidderdale Museum Society
The Book of Northlew with Ashbury • Northlew
History Group
The Book of North Newton • J.C. and K.C. Robins
The Book of North Tawton • Baker, Hoare and Shields
* *The Book of Notting Hill* • Melvin Wilkinson
The Book of Nynehead • Nynehead & District
History Society
The Book of Okehampton • Roy and Ursula Radford
The Book of Ottery St Mary • Gerald Gosling and
Peter Harris
The Book of Paignton • Frank Pearce
The Book of Penge, Anerley & Crystal Palace •
Peter Abbott
The Book of Peter Tavy with Cudlipptown • Peter Tavy
Heritage Group
The Book of Pimperne • Jean Coull
The Book of Plymtree • Tony Eames
The Book of Poole • Rodney Legg
* *The Book of Porchfield & Locks Green* • Keir Foss
The Book of Porlock • Dennis Corner
* *The Book of Portland* • Rodney Legg
Postbridge – The Heart of Dartmoor • Reg Bellamy
The Book of Priddy • Albert Thompson
The Book of Princetown • Dr Gardner-Thorpe
The Book of Probus • Alan Kent and
Danny Merrifield
The Book of Rattery • By the People of the Parish
The Book of Roadwater, Leighland and Treborough •
Clare and Glyn Court
* *The Book of St Audries* • Duncan Stafford
The Book of St Austell • Peter Hancock
The Book of St Day • Joseph Mills and Paul Annear
The Book of St Dennis and Goss Moor • Kenneth Rickard
* *The Book of St Ervan* • Moira Tangye
The Book of St Levan • St Levan Local History Group
*The Book of Sampford Courtenay
with Honeychurch* • Stephanie Pouya
The Book of Sculthorpe • Gary Windeler
The Book of Seaton • Ted Gosling
The Book of Sidmouth • Ted Gosling and Sheila Luxton
The Book of Silverton • Silverton Local History Society
The Book of South Molton • Jonathan Edmunds

The Book of South Stoke with Midford • Edited by
Robert Parfitt
South Tawton & South Zeal with Sticklepath • Roy and
Ursula Radford
The Book of Sparkwell with Hemerdon & Lee Mill • Pam James
* *The Book of Spetisbury* • Ann Taylor
The Book of Staverton • Pete Lavis
The Book of Stithians • Stithians Parish History Group
*The Book of Stogumber, Monksilver, Nettlecombe
& Elworthy* • Maurice and Joyce Chidgey
The Book of South Brent • Greg Wall
The Book of Studland • Rodney Legg
The Book of Swanage • Rodney Legg
The Book of Tavistock • Gerry Woodcock
* *The Book of Thatcham* • Peter Allen
The Book of Thorley • Sylvia McDonald and Bill Hardy
The Book of Torbay • Frank Pearce
The Book of Truro • Christine Parnell
The Book of Uplyme • Gerald Gosling and Jack Thomas
The Book of Watchet • Compiled by David Banks
The Book of Wendling, Longham and Beeston with Bittering •
Stephen Olley
The Book of West Huntspill • By the People
of the Parish
The Book of Weston-super-Mare • Sharon Poole
* *The Book of Whippingham* • Sarah Burdett
The Book of Whitchurch • Gerry Woodcock
Widecombe-in-the-Moor • Stephen Woods
Widecombe – Uncle Tom Cobley & All • Stephen Woods
The Book of Williton • Michael Williams
* *The Book of Wilton* • Chris Rousell
The Book of Wincanton • Rodney Legg
The Book of Winscombe • Margaret Tucker
The Book of Witheridge • Peter and Freda Tout
and John Usmar
The Book of Withycombe • Chris Boyles
Woodbury: The Twentieth Century Revisited • Roger Stokes
The Book of Woolmer Green • Compiled by the
People of the Parish
The Book of Yetminster • Shelagh Hill
* *The Book of Veryan & Portloe* • Diana Smith and
Christine Parnell

For details of any of the above titles or if you are
interested in writing your own history, please
contact: Commissioning Editor, Community
Histories, Halsgrove House, Lower Moor Way,
Tiverton, Devon EX16 6SS, England; email:
katyc@halsgrove.com

* *2006 publications*